SCOTTISH
FOLK
TALES
OF
COAST
AND
SEA

SCOTTISH FOLK TALES

OF

COAST AND SEA

TOM MUIR

ILLUSTRATED BY
BEA BARANOWSKA

The History Press

First published 2024

The History Press
97 St George's Place, Cheltenham,
Gloucestershire, GL50 3QB
www.thehistorypress.co.uk

Text © Tom Muir, 2024
Illustrations © Bea Baranowska, 2024

British Library Cataloguing in Publication Data.
A catalogue record for this book is available from the British Library.

ISBN 978 1 80399 205 1

Typesetting and origination by The History Press
Printed and bound in Great Britain by TJ Books Limited, Padstow, Cornwall.

Trees for LYfe

DEDICATION

This collection of tales of the sea I would like to
dedicate to my brothers and sister:

Jim, Cecil, John, David
& Elizabeth Muir

In appreciation of your kindness and patience over the
years and for putting up with your feral peedie brother.

CONTENTS

ACKNOWLEDGEMENTS

Firstly, I would like to thank Nicola Guy for inviting me to write this book in the first place, and to all the staff at The History Press for making it a reality. A huge thank you to Bea Baranowska, whose artwork lifts the stories from the page.

While this was very much a book-led publication, I would like to say a very special thank you to Linda Williamson for her kind permission to let me include two of Duncan Williamson's wonderful tales, 'The Selkie's Revenge' and 'Death in a Nut'. They add so much to the book. Also, my thanks to Erin Farley for her help and permission to use the Bell Rock story from her *Angus Folk Tales*. Erin is like a daughter to me, and a fine storyteller to boot! I am also indebted to Cairistìona Stiùbhart for her help with the Gaelic in two stories.

To my family; my son Danny, his wife Amy and their beautiful little daughter, Lily. My first grandchild! To my daughter Josie and her partner Phil. To my stepchildren (although they are hardly 'children') Sarah, Luke, Bridgett and Rachel, and their significant others, from your faux pa. I want to thank you all for being in my life and for your support and love. That goes for Rhonda's family too, brothers Jeff and Dave, sister Heather and stepmother Londa, and the irrepressible Cindy, my really cool mother-in-law.

My brothers and sister I have already thanked in the dedication, but I would like to acknowledge their tremendous help and support with their own real, live Assipattle. As a dreamy dyslexic bairn, it was they who taught me, not the schools. Being supplied with comics by David helped me to learn to read, which I struggled with, and to Liz for reading to me when I was very small. I am now surrounded by books and love to write. Sadly, Cecil lost his battle with cancer in 2010, but he is still around. As are my parents, Johnny and Lizzie. As you grow older you come to realise more and more just how important, and what a blessing, your family is.

Tragically, my sister Liz didn't live to see this book as cancer took her on 9 August 2023. Her loss will be hard to bear, but she will always remain in our hearts.

Lastly, but by no means least, I would like to thank my dear, best-beloved wife, Rhonda. Without your support, as my rock in life's storms, I really don't know what I would do. You mean everything to me. Also, Rhonda is my editor and proof reader. A perfect team. I am a lucky dog!

FOREWORD

Scotland is a land defined by its seas and coasts. The indented western seaboard adds hundreds of miles of sea loch to numerous island and mainland shores. To south, east and west, the mighty firths or estuaries of Solway, Moray, Tay, Forth and Clyde define patterns of land use and settlement. To the north the Atlantic and North Sea ocean currents clash with mind-blowing force in the Pentland Firth. In Argyll, at the head of the Sound of Jura, the Corryvreckan Whirlpool, third largest in the world, is a lurking danger to the boats that ply that often balmy coast.

This makes sea and coast a major factor in people's lives and livelihoods in Scotland, and so consequently an abundant source of folklore. In this salty collection, Tom Muir nets a choice harvest of tales that can only delight storytellers, sailors, and coastal explorers alike. There are some classic favourites here but also lots of fresh catches, with the various supernatural creatures of the sea interacting with long-suffering and sometimes lucky humans.

Tom Muir is a storyteller and folklorist based in his native Orkney. He combines those two roles with a special passion that leads him to excellent story sources, and a respectful determination to deliver traditional tales to fresh hearers. To do this, Tom resists embellishments of story or performance. He has a gift for conveying the clear lines and the heart of a tale in a direct no-nonsense fashion. But that tone is firmly grounded in his own understanding, his unique voice as an Orkney storyteller who has gone out into the world, like a seafarer, to share and gather tales from many nations connected by the sea.

There is no better guide to the stories of Scotland's seas and coasts than Tom Muir. In this book he opens up a theme that is more relevant to our shared global future than ever before. I feel sure that this fine collection will be followed by more voyages of discovery.

Donald Smith
Director
Scottish International Storytelling Festival

INTRODUCTION

The coastline of Scotland, which takes in every island, great and small, is a place steeped in lore. It is a liminal space, between sea and land, and those who live there must be careful of the supernatural as well as the physical world. The folk tales that have grown up along the coast reflect not only the old beliefs of our ancestors, they also reflect the migration of peoples. Scotland was never a country with only one ethnic group. Waves of invaders and settlers brought with them their own cultures and stories. In the west we find that connection with Ireland, which is reflected in the tales. In the northern Isles and north Scotland, the Vikings brought stories and songs that mingled with an older tradition. In the east, in what was the homeland of the Picts and Anglo-Saxons, the tales have their own flavour. Some areas have more sea tales than others, which was frustrating when trying to represent the eastern Central Belt and Borders. I hope their people will forgive my failure.

I was born by the sea, and it has always been an important part of my life. While I didn't make my living from it, the sea shapes the lives and destiny of all islanders. It seeps into every cell in your body; that connection cannot be denied or ignored. There is something much deeper than just affection. The sea calls to you and you miss it when you are away from it for any length of time. In times of sorrow, I head to the sea to draw solace from the sound of its lapping waters. It is a balm for the soul. The sight of huge breakers smashing against the rocks is a constant fascination for me and many hours could be spent watching them.

But you must never underestimate its power: I lost an uncle to the waves long before I was born, and a dear friend. The sea can be cruel and unforgiving, as you will see in some of these tales. They contain a wide pantheon of supernatural beings, from the dangerous Blue Men of the Minch and the jealous mermaid to the gentle selkie folk who live between two worlds. I hope that my selection and retelling of these stories will meet with your approval, like the warm sea washing a sandy beach, and not with the fury of an Atlantic wave crashing against a cliff.

Tom Muir, May 2023

EAST AND NORTH COASTS

THE THREE QUESTIONS

Fife

In the Kingdom of Fife, there once lived a fisherman called Davie, and his wife Maggie. Their home was a wee cottage by the sea and Davie scratched a living from the deep. He had become a fisherman when he was just a boy, but that was not of his own choosing. In fact, if the truth be told, Davie hated the sea, and he hated his job. He would never be competent enough to buy his own boat, that was for sure, so he used to hire himself on whatever fishing boat would have him. All the local skippers got to know his reputation as a man of limited use on the sea, so work was scarce.

One day, as Davie was out at sea, the net was hauled and the fish cascaded onto the deck. It was Davie's job to sort out the catch and to throw back the undersized fish, so that they could grow and be caught again. Then he had to start gutting them, a cold, dirty and smelly job that Davie hated most of all. This was always his lot on board a fishing boat. He got the dirty and menial tasks that the more accomplished men disdained to do.

Davie started to throw the small fish over the side of the boat. This was the only thing that he liked to do, to spare the life of another living creature. As he was doing this, a large fish wriggled its way towards the top of the pile. Davie stood stock-still, staring at it. It looked like a mackerel, with the distinctive blue and black stripy pattern along its back and sides, while the rest of it was silver. But this could not be a mackerel, because it was at least four times as big as one of those.

It had such a beautiful look about it that Davie felt compelled to spare its life, like he had spared the life of the small fish. He had a quick look around and saw that the skipper and the rest of the crew were too busy to see what he was up to. Davie picked up that large fish and he tossed it over the side of the boat and into the sea with a splash. He saw the fish dive down into the depths of the sea, then it was gone.

But Davie had been seen, and soon the skipper was standing in front of him, shouting and swearing at him. Davie was told that he was not paid to throw away valuable fish, and that once back in port he could go to a warmer place than on that boat. Not only that, but the skipper said that he would spread the word and Davie would be lucky if he ever got a job linked to the fishing trade for the rest of his life.

Sure enough, on reaching port Davie was kicked off the boat with no wages, but with his reputation in tatters. What would he do now? What would Maggie say when he told her that he was finished in the area? It was a very sad and sorry Davie who slowly walked home that evening.

As Davie trudged on along the road nursing his misery, he became aware that he was not alone. A stranger had fallen into step with him and was now keeping step with him by his side. The stranger was a tall, good-looking man, and he was leading a black and white cow by a rope around its neck. Davie was too depressed to pay much attention to the man, which was something he regretted later. Had he looked a bit closer he might have noticed his feet. He didn't have any! Just a pair of hooves, while on his head there grew a pair of horns. But Davie didn't notice any of those things.

Then the stranger spoke. 'It's in low spirits you are this evening, Davie.'

'Aye,' sighed Davie, 'I don't have my troubles to look for. I've lost my job on a fishing boat and it looks like it might have been my last one, too. I don't know what to do, or what to tell my Maggie.'

'Ach, that's an awful shame, Davie,' said the stranger, 'but I might be able to help you out. You see this cow here? Oh, she's a fine beast! She gives so much milk and cream that you and your wife could make butter and cheese to sell, along with the milk. I'll tell you what I'll do: as I am a fair man, I'll let you borrow my cow for three years, but after that time I'll return to collect her. I will ask you three questions and if you can give me an answer to them, then the cow is yours to keep.'

'And if I don't?'

'Well, if you don't then you'll belong to me.'

Davie started to feel uneasy, but he was desperate.

'Okay, you have yourself a deal! Oh, by the way, what's your name?'

'The Devil,' he said, then vanished in a puff of smoke.

It was a very sheepish Davie who had to explain to Maggie about losing his job and his soul, all in just one day. But she remained remarkably cheery about the situation. She had been married to Davie for long enough to be familiar with disappointments in life.

'Well Davie, we have three years to turn our fortunes around and maybe we can figure out an answer to the Devil's questions too. I'm off to milk the cow.'

Maggie milked the beast, which had a very different temperament from its previous owner. She stood as still as a rock while Maggie filled buckets and pots and pans with milk. She had never seen a cow give so much rich, creamy milk before.

'Davie, my lad, we will make a fortune with this cow. You know, I have always had a dream. I have always wanted to open a nice little tearoom. With the milk, cream, butter and cheese from this cow, we can make that dream a reality.'

So, Maggie made butter and cheese to sell in the market, and she always had the finest milk to sell as well. Soon they had enough money to buy a small tearoom that Maggie could call her own.

Business boomed, and before long they were as rich as the milk. But time doesn't stand still, and eventually the three years were up. Davie had lost track of the date when he had entered into the deal with the Devil until late one day the door opened and in stepped Auld Nick himself. He was looking pleased with himself. He looked around the teashop and saw that Davie only had the one customer, who was sitting quietly at a table in the corner.

The Devil laughed and fixed Davie with his stare, saying, 'I've come for my cow, and I have my three questions to ask you. Are you ready, Davie?'

Before Davie could open his mouth, the stranger who was sitting in the corner said, 'Aye, Davie's ready. And that's your first question.'

The Devil was taken aback by this, then his temper began to flare up, and he said, 'Will you mind your own business?'

'No, I won't,' said the stranger, 'and that's your second question.'

By this time the Devil was raging, and he roared, 'Who is this interfering busybody?'

The stranger calmly looked the Devil square in the face and said, 'I am the King of the Fish. Three years ago, Davie spared my life, and I have come here today to repay my debt to him. And that was your third question!'

The Devil was so consumed with a passionate rage that he stamped his hoof on the floor, leaving a mark on the polished flagstone. He disappeared in a great cloud of smoke and brimstone. He left in such a hurry that he forgot to take the cow with him, who continued to give the best milk to Maggie and Davie for the rest of their days.

THE BELL ROCK

Angus

Henry, the Abbot of Arbroath Abbey, sat in his high seat, deep in thought. His thoughts were the same ones that had been with him his whole life. He thought of the treacherous reef that stood eleven miles out to sea, called the Inchcape Rock. It had been the cause of so much misery and suffering, as ship after ship fell victim to it. So many ships torn to pieces on its jagged teeth, so many lives cut short, so many families left grieving for their loved ones who would no longer return to them.

Henry knew that feeling all too well. His own father had perished on the rock while on his way home to his wife and newborn son. Henry had never met his father, as he was away serving in the army when Henry was born. His mother was so broken-hearted by the loss of her much-beloved husband that she gave the huge estate that had belonged to her father to the abbey, along with the care of her fatherless child.

She knew that she could not survive the grief she bore, and that death was waiting for her, ready to take her to be reunited with her lost love. The baby boy grew up not knowing his parents, cloistered away with only monks for a family. He gave himself up to do God's work, taking holy orders and rising to become abbot.

But he often thought of the rock that had robbed him of so much in life. If only there was a way to stop it in its devilish work.

The abbey at Arbroath was dedicated to the martyred archbishop, Thomas Becket. Prayers were sent up each day for the sake of his soul. The abbey was built near to the coast, and the local villagers were poor fisherfolk. The sea was both a giver and a taker, for it provided the means to make a living and food to eat, but it also claimed the lives of many of those who toiled on it. The abbey tried to help those sailors by lighting the large, round window that faced the sea, high up in the south transept. The 'Round O', as it was called locally, acted as a beacon to sailors after the hours of darkness, when the abbey itself was no longer visible.

One day, Henry ordered a boat to be made ready to go to sea. He ordered the men to take the boat as close as they could to Inchcape Rock, so that he could look at it. It was a calm day, and the tide was low, so he landed on the rock without much trouble. Fragments of broken ships were to be seen wedged between the crevices in the rocks. The danger of the rock was apparent for all to see. Now Henry had a plan. He returned with building materials, day after day, to labour on the taming of the reef that had stolen his parents from him. His plan was to have a bell erected on the island, so precisely balanced on its stand that the slightest breeze or surging wave would cause it to ring out a warning to any mariners who were sailing in the vicinity.

At last, a fine bronze bell was cast, ready to take up its solitary post. Henry had the bell brought to the rock, and it was suspended from the sturdy stand that would hold it. The Inchcape Rock now had a voice that would save many lives with its warning cry. The work ended on 29 December, the feast day of Saint Thomas Becket, which Henry saw as a good omen. Soon, the tolling of the bell warned sailors that the Inchcape Rock was nearby, and they could take evasive action to avoid it. The sailors who passed it now gave it a new name. They called it the Bell Rock.

While the sailors sent up a prayer to Abbot Henry for his charitable deeds, not all mariners were so gracious. No one was more depraved than Ralph Vandergroot, known as Ralph the Rover. He was a notorious Dutch pirate who raided shipping in the North Sea. His heart was empty of pity, but full of greed. He regarded human life as a mere nothing, and he murdered and plundered without mercy.

One day, Vandergroot's ship sailed by the Bell Rock. It was low tide, and the deadly reef was exposed. Vandergroot ordered the ship to go as close as possible to the rock, as he wanted to see the now-famous bell. The boat was brought close in until it touched the rock, and the captain stepped ashore. He walked over to the bell and examined it with interest. He saw that it was made of the finest bronze, which was a valuable metal, and he decided to take it. He ordered his men to help, and the bell was removed from its stand and brought on board the pirate ship.

The ship's second-in-command was a man called Jan Hanson. He watched with horror and disbelief as Vandergroot had the bell carried on board. 'Captain,' he said, 'you cannot steal that bell. It was set up by holy men, with the blessings of saints and God Almighty. If you take that bell, then great misfortune will follow.'

'I never had you down as superstitious, Hanson,' sneered the captain. 'I will not tolerate that on my ship.'

'Then set me ashore in Arbroath,' said Hanson. 'I will not stay on this ship with that bell.'

Vandergroot's faced flushed red with fury, and he roared, 'You are free to leave this ship whenever you like, Hanson!'

So saying, he sprang at Hanson and seized hold of him, lifting him bodily off the deck and tossing him over the side of the ship before the poor man knew what was happening. Like most sailors in those days, Hanson couldn't swim. It was only thought to prolong the suffering. He sank, then rose again. As he broke the surface of the water he fixed the captain with a stare, saying,

'You'll see me again!' And then he disappeared under the water for good.

Vandergroot was unmoved by what had happened. He made a point of not becoming too attached to any of his crewmen. They returned home to Amsterdam, where Vandergroot had the bell erected in the garden of his home, like a trophy for misdeeds.

A year or more passed, and Vandergroot found himself approaching the Angus coast once again. The winter weather had been poor all day, but now a storm was gathering from the west. The wind rose, the rain lashed down in slanting sheets and the waves grew higher. Soon the ship was pitching and tossing wildly. The sun set and darkness fell; they had no idea where they were. Thunder roared above their heads and lightning flashed. The 'Round O' of Arbroath Abbey could be seen in the distance, which meant the rock must be nearby. But where?

A flash of lightning lit up the deck, and there stood Jan Hanson, his clothes dripping wet and seaweed tangled in his hair. He laughed, although it was more like a high-pitched shriek than a laugh, and it seemed to mix with the sound of the screaming wind. The captain stared at him in horror, then the ghostly figure spoke.

'Vandergroot, you will sleep with me this night.'

No sooner were the words out of his mouth than there was an almighty crash as the ship struck the hidden Bell Rock. Timbers were splintered and masts fell in the carnage of the wreck. The sea and wind were relentless as they ground the ship to pieces on the treacherous rocks. Vandergroot and all his men perished on that night. It was 29 December, the feast day of Saint Thomas Becket.

At home in Amsterdam, Vandergroot's wife was having a social gathering for friends and neighbours. The gale that was raging off the coast of Arbroath had not yet reached Holland, which was experiencing a relatively calm evening. Suddenly, Mrs Vandergroot heard the sound of the bell in her garden starting to ring loudly. Surprised by this, she went outside to investigate. There she saw the figure of Jan Hanson, his clothes dripping with water, and seaweed tangled in his hair, ringing the bell wildly with an evil smile on his face.

THE BLACKTHORN STICK

Aberdeenshire

There was once a wee fishing village on the east coast of Scotland, just north of Aberdeen. I don't know if it is still there or not, for this story happened a long time ago.

The fishermen of the village were very proud of their boats, and who could blame them? The boat was not only a status symbol but also the means by which they made their living. Younger lads with no boat of their own would hire themselves out to a man who did own one. They took a share of the catch, but the largest portion went to the owner. And the boat got its own share too, for its upkeep and maintenance.

There was one young lad who had a fine boat. Oh, it wasn't the biggest or the best boat in the harbour, but to him it was the most beautiful, because he owned it. It wasn't a new boat, but it was solidly built and handled well at sea. The young fisherman had a small crew compared to most boats, but they worked hard and had money to spend, or to save for their own boat one day. The fisherman had a sweetheart, and he loved her every bit as much as he loved his boat. She was a bonnie lass, but she also possessed wisdom and was known for being level-headed. She could think her way through any trouble in a way that the young laddie could not. He knew that if they had a good fishing season then he'd have enough money to marry her and to provide a wee house for them to call their own.

But things didn't work out the way that the young fisherman had planned. The boats left the harbour with the dawn, heading for their fishing grounds in the North Sea. The sun was shining and the weather was mild as the boats sailed further and further away from the coast. But the weather can change quickly, and that is what happened on this day. The dark clouds started to gather and the wind rose, swinging around to the north, bitingly cold, blowing from the Arctic. The wind grew stronger and the sea started to swell, with large waves forming. The cold sea spray lashed the faces of the fishermen as they tried to turn their boats back to shore. It was clear to them all: a storm was coming that would claim lives.

The young fisherman gave the order to turn the boat, but it was too late. The storm hit them with its full fury. The sea roared and the wind howled as the boats started to turn. One was caught by a strong gust and capsized, much to the horror of the young men in the boat. There was no way that they could turn the boat back to try to save the crew in the water. They had to hope that one of the other boats could reach them before the cold sea claimed them.

Another boat was swamped by a huge wave and struggled to keep afloat. The young fisherman used all his skills to save his boat and the crew, but luck was not on his side that day. A mountainous wave struck the small boat like an enormous hammer, splintering wood and turning it right over. The young fisherman found himself being sucked down, struggling to kick off his boots in order to stay afloat. His head broke the surface and he gasped for breath. The cold was unbearable; his life seemed to be at its end already. He thought of his sweetheart, so loving and kind, and called her name, almost as though he was saying goodbye.

Then he felt himself being grabbed by several hands, and he was pulled into another boat. He lay there, more dead than alive, as the boat struggled against the storm and headed towards the safety of the harbour. The men who had rescued him brought him home to his parents' house. His mother wept as she stripped him and dried him and laid him in the bed. Memories of her mother doing this for her father flooded into her mind, and they were bitter to bear. The cold had reached her father's vital organs. He hadn't pulled through.

But the lad was strong and his love for his sweetheart may have made the difference, because he recovered. His mother and his own dear sweetheart tended him with loving care while he slowly grew stronger. But while his body was healed, his mind and his heart were broken. He knew that he was lucky to be alive. Many families mourned the loss of their sons, fathers and brothers who were not so fortunate, but his beloved boat was splintered and had sunk to the bottom of the unforgiving sea. Without a boat, how could he marry his love? He had no house to shelter her and no boat to provide an income to support her. He could see no way out of this tragedy that had befallen him.

His mother said that he should marry her anyway, and they could live with her and his father, but he thought that was unfair on them. His sweetheart said that they could wait a while until they saved their money and were able to wed. Seeing his despair, his sweetheart, who was a wise and level-headed girl, proposed another plan. Instead of him moping around the harbour lamenting the loss of his boat, he should swallow his pride and sign on as a crewman on another fishing boat. That would at least bring in some money that they could use to get themselves established with. She would also leave the village and head inland to seek employment on one of the crofts. Little by little, they would earn enough to be able to marry. With a deep sigh, he agreed with her, his sensible girl, so strong, so supportive.

The next day, the young couple set off on the road inland. The young man was quiet and thoughtful, while the young woman was cheerful – or at least she pretended to be. They walked along until the road met the highway, and there they had to part company.

He would return to the fishing village where they were born, where they had both grown up and it had always been known that they were destined to be together. She would head inland and trust to her luck for finding work.

As they parted, he handed her a strong, sturdy blackthorn stick that he had been carrying under his arm, saying, 'It's not much of a gift to give to the one you love, but take this stick to help you on your journey and to support you, just as you have supported me.'

They kissed lovingly and he turned his back to her and returned to the coast. She picked up the bundle that contained all her worldly goods and headed inland, looking for a crofter who wanted to hire a servant lass. But as she went from croft to croft, she always got the same answer: 'We don't need a servant lass; we hired one at the fair last month.'

She had missed the hiring fair, and now all the posts were filled. As darkness fell, she saw a small shepherd's hut and she sheltered there for the night. In the morning, she dusted herself down and fixed her hair before having a wee bite to eat of the food that she had brought with her. She then went to a nearby burn and drank the cold, clear water before washing her hands and face there. With her bundle under her arm and her strong, sturdy blackthorn stick in her hand, she set off again.

All that day she walked from croft to croft, but it was always the same story. No servant lasses were needed. As the evening wore on she finally saw a large house, a bit finer than the other houses had been. It had two storeys and looked like the prosperous dwelling house of a well-to-do family. She headed up the path that led to the door, hoping for a change of luck.

Inside the house the family were gathered, covered in dust and cobwebs from their day's toil. In the front room, the old man was lying dead.

They were, indeed, a well-off family, as the girl suspected. But the old man loved his gold more than he loved his children.

They had all worked hard on the farm, but it was the father who took the sheep and cattle to the market, and it was he who came home with the money. But they never saw a penny of it. He hid it – where they did not know, but when he took ill and went to his bed the family tried to find out. When they saw that he was near to death they harassed him, constantly asking him where the money was hidden, but he just grinned and said nothing. He had died that morning, and the family had made a thorough search of the house, but without finding the hiding place.

The eldest son saw the young woman coming up the path towards the house and said, 'Look, a stranger is coming.'

'Yes, indeed,' said his wife, 'a stranger is coming. Maybe she can be of use to us.'

'Just what I was thinking,' said her husband, who looked knowingly at his brothers and their wives.

They all smiled and nodded at each other. For they knew the old tradition that had been handed down among the farming folk for generations. If someone died who had a secret, and if you asked them what you wanted to know then got a stranger to sit with the corpse all night while the outside door was ajar, then the dead would rise and tell the secret. This was the task that they wanted this stranger to do for them, but of course, they were not going to tell her about it.

When the young woman knocked on the door the eldest son answered it. She asked if he had any work, and the elder son asked her where she came from and quizzed her, to see if he could find out if she knew anything about the tradition of sitting with corpses.

Once he was sure that the girl knew nothing about it, he said, 'We don't need a servant, as there is a large enough family here to carry out the work. But,' he added, 'this is a house of grief, as our father died this very morning. We sat nursing him in his final hours and we are very tired, so we would hire you to sit up all night, watching over his body. I'll give you a gold and a silver coin as your pay.'

'Aye,' said the young woman, 'I can do that.'

Now, that was not a bad night's wages, she thought, and it was certainly better than nothing. At least she'd get something to eat and have a roof over her head. Little did she know that he had no gold or silver coin to pay her with. That all depended on her finding out the old man's secret.

The elder son smiled and said, 'The old devi– I mean, our dear father's body is in the front room. Watch over him, and I want to hear if anything happens. Not that it will, of course.'

The young woman was led to a room where a table was spread with food for her to eat. She was hungry and ate her fill. Then she was taken to the front room, where the old man's corpse lay. A fire blazed away merrily in the hearth and a comfortable chair was set facing the bed where the old man had been laid. While the young woman was not in the habit of socialising with the dead, she saw nothing to worry her. He was definitely dead, after all, and couldn't do her any harm.

The family all filed into the room after her and gathered together in a corner to whisper to each other. She had no idea what was said, but they all went, one by one, to the body of the old man and whispered something in his ear. She was touched, thinking that they were saying a prayer over their late father.

But it was no prayer. They were all saying, 'What have you done with your gold?'

The eldest son said that they were all going to bed now, as they had been up all night tending to their dying father and were exhausted. They bade her a good night and reminded her that she must stay awake and watch over him all night. Then, before going upstairs, the eldest son opened the front door and left it ajar. With a sly smile, he climbed the stairs and went to bed.

The young woman sat comfortably next to the old man's bed, her bundle beside her and her strong, sturdy blackthorn stick resting by her knee. Knowing that it had been a parting gift from her sweetheart made it a connection with him.

She was tired from all her walking that day. Her head started to nod with sleep, but she made herself stay awake. As the night wore on to midnight, the fire was burning low. The young woman went over to put another couple of logs on it. It was then that she heard a rustling sound behind her, and as she turned she saw the corpse of the old man propped upright, leaning on his elbow, and grinning at her in an awful manner.

She waved the blackthorn stick in his face and said in a stern voice, 'Och, lie down there man, or you'll feel the end of my stick on your head.' She noticed a cold, icy draught, and she turned to see where it was coming from. There was the door standing ajar, so she slammed it shut. She turned around to face the old man's corpse, but he was lying on the bed again, perfectly still. She thought that she must have been dreaming and settled back in the chair, with her blackthorn stick beside her.

In the morning, the family came down and asked her if she had seen anything during the night. She said that she had seen or heard nothing, only the door had been left ajar and she'd slammed it shut. If they had heard anything, then it would have been that. They looked disappointed, but gave her a hearty meal and showed her to her room where she could sleep for the rest of the day. They would, said the eldest, want her to sit with the corpse again that night. It would be the last time though, as it was his funeral the following day. She ate and slept, and the following evening they woke her up for her nocturnal vigil.

The fire was blazing away, and the chair was where it had been the night before. The family all filed past the old man's corpse and whispered in his ear, 'Where did you hide your gold?'

This time, when the eldest son left, he opened the front door and put a piece of wood against the hinge to prevent it from closing.

She sat there watching over the corpse and feeling relieved that it was the last night. But at midnight she heard the rustle of the bedclothes, and when she looked at him, the corpse was sitting up, propped on one elbow and grinning at her. Quick as a flash she was on her feet, brandishing the strong, sturdy blackthorn stick that her sweetheart had given to her.

'You lie down decently or I'll beat you with my stick!'

But the corpse just leered at her, grinning even wider than before. Again she felt the cold chill gripping her, and she stepped nearer to the fire to warm up. She then saw that the front door was ajar again, so she pushed it to shut it. But the piece of wood in the door jamb stopped it from closing.

'The devil take this door!' she cried. 'Why won't it shut properly?'

With that the corpse leapt out of bed and darted towards the door.

'You come back here right now, you old dead rascal,' cried the young woman, 'and lie down on your bed like a decent body!'

She set off after the corpse, swinging her blackthorn stick at him as she ran. She aimed at his backside and swung the stick, but the corpse caught it in his hand and set off at lightning speed. He wouldn't let go of that stick and neither would she, so she had to follow him.

The corpse ran for a mile down the road before turning aside and running over the moor with the young woman running behind him, still holding that blackthorn stick. They ran up hill and down dale. She struggled to keep up with him, as they ran through gorse bushes and heather. Three branches swung back and hit her in the face, but she would not let go of that blackthorn stick that her sweetheart had given her.

On and on they ran, until the early signs of dawn started to lighten the sky. Then the corpse turned and ran back home as fast as he could go. The poor young woman was exhausted, but she held on tight to that blackthorn stick. Eventually, they were running up the road towards the house once more. In through the door ran the corpse, followed by the young woman, and straight over to his bed just as the cock in the rafters of the barn started to crow.

He let go of the blackthorn stick and lay back on the bed, fixed her with a steely gaze and said in a hollow voice, 'In the chimney, under the thatch it is. But if you had let go of that stick, I would have told you nothing!'

Then he closed his eyes and crossed his arms over his breast and was still. He looked so peaceful that you would never know that he had moved at all that night. The young woman tidied her hair and straightened her skirts and sat back in the chair, her stick by her knee, and waited for the household to arrive.

It was the eldest son's wife who was the first to come in. When she saw the old man's corpse lying peacefully on the bed and saw the young woman sitting there quietly, she began to weep and wail.

'Och, the old man's secret will go to the grave with him if he didn't tell you where his money is hidden last night, for we bury him today.'

The young woman's eyes were now turned from the flames of the fire towards the housewife. She knew that she had been used by them for their own ends, and she didn't like being used. Her eyes hardened and she said, 'Quit your jabbering, woman. I've had a hell of a night with your old man there. But in the end he told me his secret.'

Then she told the eldest son's wife all about her night and the chase that she had, up hill and down dale, across moors and through heather, bracken, gorse and woods.

'But he told me his secret in the end, though.'

'Oh, mercy! You know what his secret was then?'

'Aye, I do.'

'Then, for God's sake, tell it to me.'

The young woman was clever, and not only that, she was offended by her treatment. They had tricked her, deceived her, left her to face a walking corpse alone. She knew that what they had done to her was worth more than one piece of gold and one piece of silver.

'No, I don't think it's right to tell you. He told it to me, but I feel that I should respect his confidence. If he'd wanted you lot to have his gold, then he would have told you himself when he was alive. His secret can go to the grave with him.'

The housewife now raged at her. She wept, she cursed, she begged and wheedled, but with no success. The eldest son and his brothers and sisters-in-law came in to see what the news was.

'She knows, but she won't tell us!' screamed the housewife.

They shouted, they cursed, they begged and grovelled. They apologised for the danger they had put her in, until finally the eldest son said to her, 'I'll make a deal with you. We have searched high and low and we can't find a single penny of the old man's fortune, and he had many years gathering it, so it must be quite a tidy sum. Maybe we could give you a bit more than we first offered. What do you say?'

'I'll think about it,' she said.

After a while she was asked what she felt was a fair deal, and she said, 'I think that I deserve a lot more than your measly offer. I think that if I got ten pieces of gold for every hundred you found, and the same with the silver, then that would be a fair payment. Otherwise, you'll never find it, and it won't do you any good.'

The eldest son was furious, as were the others, but eventually they cooled down when they saw that she wasn't going to budge an inch.

'All right then,' said the eldest son, 'ten pieces of gold and silver for every hundred pieces we find. Do we have a deal?'

The girl said nothing.

'Well?' shouted the eldest son.

She was in no hurry, and turning towards him slowly she said, 'I'm thinking it over.'

After she thought that she had made them sweat for long enough she said, 'I will tell you nothing until you fetch a pen and paper and write down what we agreed, ten pieces from every hundred. I want it in writing and signed by you all.'

The eldest son ran to fetch the paper and pen. He wrote out the agreement and they all signed it. They handed her the paper and said, 'Well, where did he hide the money?'

'Hold on just a minute,' said the young woman, 'I have to read this first, to make sure that you haven't tried to trick me, again!' She read it, smiled, and then folded the paper and put it in her pocket.

Then she turned to the eldest son and said, 'In the chimney, under the thatch.'

Soon all the family were tearing at the thatch until they uncovered a secret door that they didn't know was there. It was so well hidden that they would never have found it by searching alone. They opened the door and saw shelves with bags of gold and silver coins. They took them down and spread them out on the table, one bag at a time. They counted out a hundred, from which they took ten pieces for the young woman. Once they had finished counting, her pile amounted to a considerable sum of money. She made sure to count it first, before she agreed that it was fair. Then she asked for a strong bag, which they happily gave her, and she filled it with her fortune. She nodded politely to them then left the house and headed back towards the coast.

After walking for a day, she arrived back at the wee fishing village where she had been born. As she walked down towards the harbour she saw a familiar sight. Her sweetheart was sitting there, staring out to sea. He had lost the two most important things in his life. First he lost his boat and then he had lost his love. He had realised that she was worth more to him than a boat or a house. She meant everything to him, and now she was away trying to make a few coins to put towards their future. He was so deep in thought that he didn't see her approach until she sat down next to him and dropped a large and heavy bag in his lap.

'Your fortune!' she said. 'Enough to buy a new boat and to build a house.'

He jumped to his feet, dropping the bag on the ground, and swept her up in his arms. 'Oh, my own true love! What do I care about boats and houses if I don't have you.'

'Well, you have it all now,' she said. 'You can have a fine new boat built and also a fine house. I have taken care of all of those things, just like I said I would.'

The two of them were married soon after, and he did have a new boat built. It was the biggest and the finest fishing boat in the village. They also had a house built, which was bigger and finer than the others. But despite their riches they carried on just as they had before.

As the years went by, the young woman had a family. She used to tell them, and her grandchildren after that, the story about her night with the miser's corpse and that strong, sturdy blackthorn stick that her sweetheart had once given her.

JOHN REID AND THE MERMAID

Ross and Cromarty

In the late 1600s, a young man called John Reid left his native town of Cromarty to go to sea. He was hired as a ship's boy, but he worked hard and soon rose through the ranks. It was a hard life, but it was just what a young lad with a thirst for adventure craved.

He sailed from the West Indies to the East Indies, around the Pacific Ocean and to China. After fourteen years he returned home with enough money and experience to buy a large sloop and to engage in trade across the North Sea between Holland and the north of Scotland.

Now, John was a cool-headed, sensible man, shrewd and calculating but not lacking in good humour, and with luck to match. He seemed to have everything that a man could wish for and yet he was deeply unhappy. Why was he unhappy? Well, her name was Helen Stuart, and she was gorgeous.

John had first clapped eyes on Helen when he was out for a solitary walk among the Cromarty hills. The vision of loveliness that John beheld made his heart jump up inside his breast and skip a beat. She was twelve years younger than he was, petite and elegant with refined, regular features and skin as white as alabaster, tinged with the pinkness of a wild rose's petals. John Reid was smitten by the sight of her, and he fell in love with her within the beat of a heart. But then that same heart turned to lead inside his breast and sank down to his boots. How on earth could he ever hope to win the love of such a divine creature as Helen Stuart? Why would she even look twice at him? He returned to his home and spent a fitful night dreaming of the beautiful lady who, unbeknown to her, was the owner of his heart.

Helen was not entirely ignorant of the existence of John Reid, whom she knew as a man of around thirty who had just returned from years at sea. He was broad-shouldered yet not very tall, and his skin was tanned to a bronze hue by the tropical sun. He looked good-natured, but then again, she had never given him a second thought. He was certainly not the stuff of fairy tales or romantic ballads, nor the sort of man who could win the affections of a young woman who had not yet given marriage any serious thought. Helen was an heiress, so financial security was not an issue for her.

John sailed back and forth between Holland and Scotland, growing his wealth with every trip but still lacking the treasure that he most desired. There was a gaping hole in his soul and only one person who could make it whole again. After a long time, which seemed like years to John, he sailed back into Cromarty Harbour one day in late April. Soon it would be May Day. He decided to climb the hillside slopes in the hope of seeing Helen and her young friends as they washed their faces in the early morning dew.

Before first light on May Day, John rose and dressed hurriedly, ready to climb the hill for the chance to see his love. The darkness was fading as he walked the rising cliffs eastwards along the coast. The sun rose red and gold from the waters of the Cromarty Firth, tinting the waves with a splash of radiant colour like a path of fire leading to the shore.

As he walked along, he neared the Dropping Cave, a place of fear and dread for all the local folk. It was a place where the supernatural met the everyday world. John couldn't see it yet, as the stony ground rose to hide it from view. He had only thoughts of Helen and whether their paths would cross. As he climbed the cliffs he heard a sound that made him stop and listen. It was a low voice singing, like the surge of the sea swell. He looked around to see if a boat was passing by or a shepherd was singing on the hillside, but there was no sight of another living soul. All that he could see was the head of a large seal, bobbing in the water and gazing intently towards the source of the music.

As he got a bit nearer John saw that the song came from a young woman, sitting on a rock near the mouth of the cave. Her voice seemed to echo back to her from the depths of the cave, like another singer was taking up her song. The lower half of her body was in the water. The white skin of her back and shoulders could be seen beneath her long, yellow hair. As she sang, the sunlight shone brightly upon her, showing the glint of a mirror in her hand.

And a patch of silver glistened beneath her waist, for there was her fish's tail shining in the morning light. She was a mermaid.

John's heart began to pound. He had spent many years at sea, and he knew all about mermaids and the dangers that they held. But he also knew that if you could overpower a mermaid then she must grant you three wishes in return for her freedom. Very quietly, he started to descend the slope towards where the mermaid sat. The rock was not far out to sea, and he knew that he could reach it without any trouble. She had her back to him as he approached, as silent as a fish's breath.

Her song turned into a scream as John grabbed her. She tried to leap into the sea, but John had her around the waist. He found that she was every bit as strong as he was, and she almost dragged him into the water, but he thought of Helen and redoubled his efforts. She struggled, but he held her tight, firmly pinned to the rock. Then her body relaxed, and she looked at him and spoke. Her voice, although as sweet as a songbird, had a cold chill to it that made the blood freeze in his veins. He knew the answer that he must give to win what he desired.

'Man, what with me?'

'Wishes three!'

John then stated what he wanted. His father had been a sailor too, but had been drowned many years before. His first wish was that neither he nor any of his family or friends would lose their lives to the sea. Knowing that Helen enjoyed plenty of wealth, his second wish was that all his ventures would succeed, and that good luck would always follow him. His third wish? Well, I don't need to tell you what that was. The mermaid heard his demands and then said: 'Quit, and have.'

John released his hold on the mermaid, who raised herself up on her tail. She looked at him, raising her hands and pressing the palms together with the edge of them before her face, then she sprang into the sea, sending spray into the air that caught the rays of the rising sun. The mermaid's white skin and silver tail glinted through the green depths of the water, and then she was gone.

John wiped the sweat from his brow. He climbed the slope back to the path and continued his walk. To his delight, he saw Helen Stuart with a lady friend, sitting on a small green mound near the cliff known as Lover's Leap. He approached them, bowing politely.

Helen's friend laughed slightly and said, 'Well, if it isn't Captain Reid, the very man that we most wish to see. Helen has just told me of the strangest dream that she had last night. In fact, we thought that it might come true not half an hour ago. See if you can read its meaning for us.'

John looked confused and said that he would do his best but that he could promise nothing.

'Helen had just fallen asleep when she dreamt that she was sitting on a grassy slope, covered with primroses and cuckoo flowers, which lies to the west of the Dropping Cave. She had been occupied in gathering the May dew, as we have been this morning, but the grass and bushes were dry, so she had only collected a few drops. She heard singing and looked down to the shore where she saw you lying asleep. A beautiful lady was sitting beside you, watching you, and singing this most enchanting song. She turned again to the bushes, but they were still dry. She felt unhappy as she thought that she would not gather any more dew. She was unhappy too that the strange lady might bewitch you to sleep until the tide covered you. The next thing that she knew you were standing beside her, and you reached over and helped her to shake the bush, which was now covered with dew. She looked to see the lady, but saw her far out to sea, floating on the waves like a seagull. Her attention was drawn to the tinkling of the dewdrops that were filling her pitcher, and every drop was now pure gold. But that is not the end of it. As we were walking here, we heard the same song from Helen's dream coming from the rocks below.

And now here you are too, to fill our pitchers with gold. You are quite like a genie from a fairy tale.'

'So, you heard the music from among the rocks,' said John, 'but I too have heard it, and I conversed with the musician. The strange, unearthly lady from Helen's dream: I have travelled the globe and sailed over almost every ocean, but I have never before beheld a mermaid.'

'Seen a mermaid?' exclaimed Helen in disbelief.

'Seen and spoken with a mermaid?' said her companion.

'Heaven forbid!' cried Helen. 'The last time that she appeared among the rocks at the Dropping Cave was only a few days before the terrible storm in which your father was lost. Take care that you do not repeat her words, for they spell doom to those who carry tales from the other world to this.'

'But I am the creature's master and need not be afraid.'

John then told them the story of his encounter with the mermaid. Helen listened with a feeling of wonder and admiration for this sailor man, and she realised that she liked him more than she had once thought. On their way home she took his arm as they passed the Dropping Cave.

Within the year they were married, and their future was as happy and as successful as anyone could have ever wished for it to be.

WHY THE SEA IS SALT

Caithness

At the time when Christ was just a child, there was a king of Denmark called Frodi Fridleifsson. During the reign of King Frodi there was a huge quern stone found in his realm. He ordered that it should be brought back to his castle, which it was, and with no small degree of effort. His men couldn't imagine what he wanted it for, as it was too large for anyone to turn. Were there not enough mills in Denmark already?

Sometime later, King Frodi went to visit his friend, King Fjolnir of Sweden. While he was at the Swedish king's court, Frodi saw that there were two giant maidens, Fenia and Menia, who were King Fjolnir's slaves. King Frodi was able to buy them and take them back to his own castle in Denmark.

He led Fenia and Menia to the room where the great quern stone, whose name was Grotti, stood in the middle of the room. He set them to their task of turning the huge quern stone around and around, like they were grinding corn into flour. But this was no ordinary quern, for it was magic and could grind out whatever the owner ordered it to. King Frodi ordered that they grind out gold, until his castle was bursting at the seams with it.

Once he had enough gold, he ordered the giants to grind out something else, something that you couldn't see but you could feel the benefit from. He bade them to grind out peace and plenty for the land, and so they did as they were commanded. It became a golden age, known as the Peace of Frodi, where good luck abounded. There were no more wars or fighting, not even an argument between anyone. The crops grew so that every stalk was bent under the weight of the ears of corn, and the branches of the trees bent under the weight of fruit. All the cows and sheep had twin offspring and there were so many fish in the sea that you could practically walk from Denmark to Norway or Sweden on the backs of them. Everyone was happy and content.

Well, not everyone was happy. Fenia and Menia had to constantly turn the quern stone to grind out everyone else's happiness and prosperity. At last they grew tired of their toil and asked King Frodi if they could have a rest. The king refused, saying that they could only rest for as long as the cuckoo can hold its peace or for as long as it takes to sing a song.

Fenia and Menia were not happy with this reply, so they composed a song. The song, which was called 'The Lay of Grotti', was a terrifying thing to hear. For they sang about warfare, violence, robbery, treachery, famine and disease. Soon all these things came to pass. The warning beacons burst into flame to signal the advancing armies that were harrying the land, killing all before them. The crops failed and rotted in the fields. Animals and people sickened and died. The land was blighted.

Then a sea king called Mysingr sailed into the harbour and attacked the castle, breaking its defences and killing King Frodi. He carried off much of Frodi's gold, and he also carried away Fenia and Menia and the quern stone, Grotti. They sailed away from the burning town and into the clear, open sea.

King Mysingr knew about Grotti's magic qualities, and he set Fenia and Menia to the task of grinding out salt. It was a rare and valuable substance in those faraway days. Salt flowed out from between the two quern stones and scattered over the deck. Later in the day, they asked Mysingr if he had enough salt yet, but he ordered them to grind on. They ground so hard and so fast that the salt filled the ship, until at last it sank to the bottom of the sea.

Mysingr and his men were drowned, but not Fenia and Menia, who were of the race of giants and not mortal creatures. Where the ship sank was in the Pentland Firth, between Orkney and Caithness, just east of the island of Stroma. There they remain to this day, grinding salt at the bottom of the sea. That is why the sea is salt. There is a whirlpool over the spot where they labour, called the Swelkie. The name comes from the Old Norse word *svelgr*, which means 'swallower', and this is an apt name as it swallows ships. The whirlpool is caused by the water falling through the eye at the centre of the quern stone as Fenia and Menia turn it around, grinding salt for the sea.

THE MERMAID'S CAVE

Caithness

There was once a young man in the north of Caithness who was handsome, muscular and athletic. Many a girl sighed at the sight of him as he strolled around the neighbourhood. He was good looking, and he knew it. But it was not just the Caithness lasses who were smitten with his looks, for he had been noticed by someone else. In the sea, a mermaid saw him walking along the coast and a desire burned brightly in her breast. She wanted him and she was determined that she would have him all to herself.

One day, as the young man was down at the shore, the mermaid cast her eyes on him and waited for the right moment to speak. She swam to the shore and pulled herself on top of a rock, where she started to sing. The young man was lured by the beautiful song, and when he saw the mermaid sitting there he was spellbound by her beauty. She saw that it was working. As he drew nearer she spoke to him.

'I have watched you from afar for a while, and you are pleasing to my eyes. I can make you an important man in the realm under the waves. I can make you rich beyond your wildest dreams, if you will be wed to me.'

The young man was amazed, but he was a hard-headed man and with a heart to match. The prospect of living in the sea did not appeal to him, and he told her as much. Seeing that he was not going to be won so easily, she spoke with him a bit longer. The conversation always came back to one thing – riches. He seemed to like this most of all. The mermaid knew his weakness, and with that knowledge she was sure that she would be able to capture him. She said that if he would meet her at the same place at the same hour the next day, then he would be well rewarded. Greedily, he agreed.

The next day he was there, as they had arranged, and the mermaid dropped silver coins onto the shore. The coins were old, lost in some ancient shipwreck, but they were solid silver. He thanked the mermaid and agreed to meet her again. More silver coins were given to the young man, much to his delight. Then came the gold coins, shining like the sun as they cascaded onto the beach. The man laughed like a child at the sight of them. After a short time he was indeed a rich man. But still he wouldn't go with her to her home under the waves.

The innkeeper didn't question the young man as to where the coins came from. There had been no word of a theft in the area, so why should he care as to their origin? The ale and whisky flowed and the young man, grown boastful about his wealth, was never short of drinking companions … just as long as he paid for the drink.

It was not only the innkeeper who benefited, for despite the young man's hardness of heart towards the mermaid, he had an eye for the earthly lasses. The trinkets that she gave to him were soon to be seen around the necks and wrists of the local girls, and jewel-encrusted gold rings decorated many slender fingers.

The mermaid was growing impatient with the young man. Why wouldn't he surrender himself to her charms? Mermaids are always on the lookout for a human husband and she wanted no other than this young man. Suspicion started to fill her thoughts and cloud her mind. She decided that she had to keep a closer eye on the young man and his activities.

Floating out at sea, she could watch him as he wandered along the coast. Mermaids have wonderful eyesight, so she could see him while he could not see her. She started to notice that, as often as not, he was not alone. There was always a girl with him. Her anger rose when she saw him hold one of them in his arms and kiss her. But her temper grew hotter still when she saw the glint of gold passing between them. How the girl gazed in wonder at the gift before putting it on. He was giving away *her* treasure to the local girls! She had seen enough, and swam away. Already she was plotting her revenge.

The next time they met she pretended that nothing had changed. Would he come and live with her under the waves? No, not yet, the time wasn't right, he said. She then asked him to kiss her. She had never asked that before. He leant over and kissed her on the lips. Oh, such a cold kiss it was.

She smiled and said, in a casual tone of voice, 'Of course, these few trinkets that I have given you are a mere nothing compared to what I have gathered.'

'Oh, you have more?'

'Why, of course. More than you could ever dream of. I keep it hidden in a cave. You see, I have all the treasure from all the ships that have ever sunk in the Pentland Firth.'

Then, with a sly smile, she turned her head on one side and said, 'Would you like to see it?'

Well, of course he did! His head spun with the thought of all the riches that lay in that cave. She led him along the shore until they came to Dwarwick Head, near Dunnet. There was a cave down by the shore, linked to the sea. He had never seen it before, yet that strange thought didn't trouble him. It should have.

He followed the mermaid into the cave and, oh! The wonders! The cave was indeed filled with all the treasures that had ever been lost in the Pentland Firth. Gold and silver and jewels were piled up in mounds. It was unbelievable!

As the man was staring in disbelief, picking up handfuls of gems and letting them run through his fingers, the mermaid smiled. It was not a smile of joy, but of satisfaction. The young man should have noticed this, and have been worried, but he was too preoccupied with the treasure.

It started softly, at first, that song. It was as soft as a lullaby, growing in sweetness as she sang. His head started to drop onto his chest, but he would shake his head and carry on lusting after the riches. The song grew in intensity, until weariness swept over him and he had to sit down and rest. The song coiled around him, filling his senses until he fell into a deep sleep.

How long he slept, he didn't know, but when he woke up he found himself lying on a rock, stiff and cold. He tried to move, but something stopped him. As his eyes grew used to the darkness that now filled the cave, he found that he was fettered. He was bound to the rock by a golden chain. At his feet sat the mermaid. She gazed at him, saying nothing. The jealousy she had felt was passing, for now she had him. Never again would he give away her treasures to mortal girls. She would keep him and guard him in that cave, filled with the treasures that his heart had so desired. And he would be there with her until the end of time.

THE SEAL HUNTER

Caithness

There was once a man who lived in a small house by the shore near John o' Groats. He made his livelihood through hunting the seals that lived around the coast and selling their skins. A well-tanned seal skin could fetch good money, and the seal hunter was well off by the standards of working people at that time. The old folks warned him that he should never hunt the large grey seals, for they were of the selkie folk, who could remove their skins and take human form. The seal hunter just laughed at them and pointed out that those large skins brought him more money than the skins of the smaller harbour seals. The old folks tutted, shook their heads and said that maybe one day he would learn his lesson, the hard way.

One fine sunny day the hunter was at the shore early, to watch for the seals landing to sun themselves. Soon they started to arrive, swimming up to the rocks near to where he lived. One was particularly large and had a finely patterned skin. The hunter's eyes widened as he thought of the value of that hide. Jackets, sea boots and purses could be made from it. He was in no hurry, as he was an experienced hunter, so he waited until the large seal settled down on a rock by the sea and fell asleep in the sun.

Slowly, the hunter took his knife in his hand and started to creep up on the sleeping seal. But just as he was about to strike, the seal woke up and saw him. The hunter lunged forward with his knife and struck the seal in its side, causing a great wound. The seal roared with pain, but managed to dive from the rock into the sea, taking the knife with it. The water was dyed red with its blood, as the hunter cursed his carelessness for losing both the seal and his good seal-killing knife.

As the other seals had taken to the water on hearing the big seal's roar, the hunter slowly walked home. He was both annoyed with himself and sad for the loss of his knife. He got home and sat by the fire and spent a few hours lost in his own thoughts. That evening, there was an unexpected knock at his door. He answered it and saw a very tall man, wearing a long, dark coat that looked like it was made out of sealskin.

The stranger asked him, 'Are you the seal hunter?'

'Yes, I am.'

'I want to place an order for two dozen skins, but I need them right away.'

'How soon?' asked the hunter, whose spirits had risen at the prospect of selling so many skins. But his heart fell when he heard the answer.

'I need them tonight.'

'But that's not possible. So many skins! The seals have left the beach and they won't return again today. I can't do it.'

'But I know a place where there are plenty of seals. I can show you. You will be able to get that many where I will take you. Come, you can ride with me on my horse.'

The hunter left his house and walked over to where the stranger's horse stood. It was as black as coal and a huge animal. Something about it made the hunter feel uneasy, but he went along all the same. The man told him to climb up behind him, and he spurred his horse into a gallop. The hunter clung on for dear life to the stranger. On and on they rode, until at last they came to a desolate clifftop, far away from his home. In fact, it was far away from anybody's home. There was not a house to be seen in any direction.

'The seals are down there,' said the stranger, pointing to indicate that they would be seen at the foot of the cliff.

As the stranger secured his horse, the seal hunter slowly moved towards the edge of the cliff and peered over. But there were no seals to be seen. There were no rocks for them to lie on, only the surge of the sea as it broke against the cliff. The hunter felt uneasy. Was this strange man going to kill him in this desolate place, far away from curious eyes? But why would he? What had he done?

In a trembling voice he said, 'I don't see any seals down there.'

'Look a bit closer,' said the stranger, who was now by his side. 'Lean forwards and look down there.'

The hunter leaned a bit further out, but to his horror, his worst suspicions were confirmed. The stranger threw his arms around him. Leaning with his whole body weight, the stranger pushed him forward. The two men fell right over the cliff edge and plummeted towards the sea. There was an almighty splash as the two men hit the water. Then the seal hunter could only hear the sound of the water rushing past his ears.

To his amazement, he wasn't choked by the water. He found that he could breathe easily underwater, as the two men shot downwards towards the seabed. Below him, he could see a large building coming closer. It seemed to be made of coral and mother-of-pearl shells, glinting softly in the hazy blue-green waters. They arrived at the great arched doorway, which opened for them, and they went inside. The floor was made of compressed yellow sand, soft to the touch. But what amazed the hunter were the inhabitants, for the place was full of seals.

He looked towards the stranger, as if for some sort of explanation. To his astonishment, the man was no longer a tall, dark stranger but a large seal. And the surprises were not over yet, for there was a large mirror hanging on the wall, and as he gazed at it, he saw that the reflection staring back at him was that of a seal. The hunter knew then that the old folks were right when they talked about the selkie folk. He had dismissed it, and now he had indeed found out the hard way.

As he looked around, it dawned on him that the seals in the building seemed unhappy. They looked sad and many had tears streaming down their faces. After a time they noticed him, and they started to whisper to each other. The stranger disappeared into a room and then returned holding something.

'Do you recognise this?' he asked, showing the hunter the lost knife.

The knife that had killed so many seals. Terror gripped him, as it became clear to him what was happening. He was being punished for the deaths of all the seals that he had killed. Now they would have their revenge on him!

'Mercy,' he cried, 'please don't kill me!'

The seals gathered around him. Looking on him with their large, gentle eyes, they started to rub their noses against him as if to reassure him.

'You have nothing to fear from us,' said that stranger. 'No harm will come to you, you have my word. But do you recognise that knife?'

'Yes, I do,' said the hunter, with a note of shame in his voice. 'I lost it this morning when I stabbed a seal.'

'Come with me,' said the stranger, and he led the hunter to the small room.

Inside the room lay a huge seal on a soft bed of pink-coloured seaweed. The seal had a gaping wound in its side where the hunter's knife had struck it.

'This is my father,' said the stranger. 'He is the king of the selkie folk. I need you to bind up the wound. Push the sides together and bandage it well.'

'But I am no healer,' protested the hunter. 'I know nothing about such things.'

'Yet you are the only one who can save him,' said the stranger.

So the seal hunter pushed the two halves of the wound together. To his amazement they stuck fast and healed, leaving only a faint scar. He bound up the place where the wound had been and the old seal opened his eyes. Great was the joy among the selkie folk once they heard the news. The hunter was then taken back into the large hall. He watched the seals as they celebrated the recovery of their king. He remained in the corner away from the others, struggling with a heavy heart. He would be doomed to live as a seal for the rest of his days.

The stranger came out of the room and went over to the hunter.

'You have done your part and can now return to your home. But before we release you, I want you to swear a solemn oath before all the gathered selkie folk. You must swear never to harm another seal for as long as you live.'

'That I will,' said the seal hunter, 'and with a right good heart!' The hunter swore a binding oath to give up his trade, and the selkie folk were overjoyed to hear it.

'Now it's time to go home,' said the stranger. 'Come with me.'

The seal hunter followed the stranger out of the great hall. He found himself travelling upwards, from the bottom of the sea to the surface. When they reached the surface they didn't stop, but shot out of the sea and up the cliff until they landed on the top of it. There was the horse, secured where the stranger had left it. The stranger was no longer a seal, but a tall man wearing a long sealskin coat. Looking down at his hands he saw that they were human again, and he wiggled his fingers in joy.

The stranger called him to mount the horse behind him, and soon they were racing back to the seal hunter's home at John o' Groats. After a short while, the horse drew up in front of the hunter's own wee cottage once more. The hunter got down and stretched his hand out to shake that of the stranger, but the man remained cool and didn't offer him his hand. Instead he dropped a large bag into the hunter's hand.

'Never let it be said that the selkie folk would deprive a man of his livelihood. There is enough there to last you for the rest of your days. Now, remember that oath that you swore, and never break it!'

With those parting words, the stranger spurred his huge black steed and rode off at great speed. The hunter went into his house and sat at his table. He opened the bag, and poured out the contents. The room lit up with a glow as a huge pile of gold coins was scattered over the top of the table. He was now a rich man, and had no need to hunt seals.

From that day on he kept his oath and never again did he harm a seal. But he would sit on the shore and watch them play together in the waters of the Pentland Firth.

THE DEVIL IN SMOO CAVE

Sutherland

The huge sea cave called Smoo lies a mile to the east of the village of Durness on the north coast of Sutherland. It has three chambers, the third only accessible by boat. There is a large hole in the roof of the second chamber through which falls the water of a stream. This creates a waterfall, which forms a pool beneath it.

There are many stories attached to this huge cave. A notorious highwayman called McMurdo used to operate in the area. Not only did he rob people of their possessions but he also robbed them of their lives. He would throw his living victims down the hole in the cave roof. It is an eighty-foot drop. Dead men tell no tales!

A piper (who had obviously not heard all the other stories about pipers who went into caves or through tunnels) decided one day to see how deep the cave ran. He set up a skirl on the pipes and walked in through its huge mouth. After a time the piping stopped, though it is said that it can still be heard sometimes, way inland.

But the most famous of all the Smoo Cave stories is that of the Wizard of Reay. This was Donald Mackay, the first Lord of Reay and the chief of the Clan Mackay, who lived from 1590 to 1649. When fighting in the Thirty Years' War (1618–48) Donald fought under the Swedish King Gustavus Adolphus. It was during this war that he first met the Devil. The two had much in common and got on well.

The Devil persuaded him that he could have more power and riches than he could find as a mercenary soldier, and offered to take him on as a student. Donald agreed and went to study under the Devil in Padua, Italy. He proved to be a good scholar and was quick to learn all of the devilish tricks that his master taught him.

But he was by no means alone in the Black School, as it was called. He was just one of many students. Once the Devil was satisfied that they had learned as much as he could teach them, he held a party. Now, it was well known to all the Devil's students that the price that had to be paid for their education was the soul of the last student to leave the classroom on the final day. That very day. They were all nervous, not wanting to risk the wrath of the Devil by leaving too early, but also not wanting to be the last to go.

Donald was a bit slow on this occasion; maybe he had drunk a few toasts too many. As the scholars ran for the door he found himself at the end of the line. Seeing the Devil looming up behind him he cried, 'De'il tak' the hindmost!'

The Devil, being rather caught off guard by this, snatched at the last person he saw leaving the room. To his fury he found himself standing there with nothing more than Donald Mackay's shadow in his hand. It was said that Donald never cast a shadow after that.

Now Donald was indeed a good scholar and he continued his studies after he got home. His reputation as a master of the black arts spread far and wide until it reached the ears of the Devil himself. His fury boiled inside of him. Donald had cheated him of a soul and now he was rivalling his power. He decided to hide in Smoo Cave and catch Donald unawares.

One evening, Donald took his dog with him as he walked around the neighbourhood. What led him to Smoo Cave I couldn't tell you, but that is where he went. It was after dark by the time master and hound reached the cave and scrambled down the steep path towards the cave's lofty entrance. He entered the first chamber but the dog ran forward into the second chamber, out of sight of Donald. The next thing that he knew came the terrible howl of the dog as it screeched with pain. The dog ran out of the second chamber, but now it had not one hair on its body. Donald knew that the Devil must be in there, waiting for him.

The feeling of dread and impending death hung over Donald, but his luck held out – a cock crowed, heralding the dawn. As the light started to gather in the east, the Devil roared and shot up into the air, breaking a hole in the roof of the cave as he went. This is the hole that the waterfall cascades through to this very day.

In another encounter, it is said, Donald found a box in the cave and made a small hole in it. A tiny man came out of the box and started to grow at an alarming rate until he was huge. Donald recognised the giant figure as the Devil, and was utterly terrified. But Donald was no fool. He'd had, after all, a good teacher. He made himself look unimpressed and maybe even slightly bored by the Devil's trick and he said, 'Any fool can make himself large, but I bet you can't make yourself small enough to fit back into that hole again.'

The Devil, whose vanity had been triggered, made himself so small that he could easily fit back into the hole in the box again. As quick as a flash, Donald shoved the tiny Devil back into the box, then took a small pebble and shoved it into the hole, sealing the Devil inside.

Another version of these two stories says that on hearing of Donald's growing power, the Devil challenged him to a fight. The two former friends clashed and a terrible fight ensued. All day long it went on until at last Donald gained the victory over his old teacher. The Devil gave him a box as a prize for his defeat.

When he opened it there was a host of tiny imps inside who swarmed out and screamed: 'Give us work! Give us work!' As they screamed they nipped, bit, kicked and punched him.

Donald set them to work pulling the heather from hilltops, but they were done with the job in no time at all. No matter what task he set them, they did it quickly and demanded more. Donald started to think that the Devil's reward was actually a curse.

One day, as he was being pestered by the imps, Donald lost his temper, and in doing so he struck upon a good idea. 'Build me a rope of sand that runs from one side of the Kyle of Tongue to the other.'

The imps dashed off to start work. No sooner had they got their rope of woven sand started, than the tide came in and washed it away. Donald waited for their return, but they never came back. He never saw the imps again, though I am sure that he and the Devil would cross paths again.

NORTHERN ISLES

THE DENSCHMAN'S HADD

Shetland

The islands of Orkney and Shetland had been Norwegian crown property since the Viking Age. In 1468, Orkney was pawned to Scotland as security for the dowry of Princess Margaret, the daughter of King Christian I of Denmark, on her marriage to King James III of Scotland. King Christian ruled both Denmark and Norway, but he didn't have the legal authority to dispose of any Norwegian territory. As his coffers remained empty, Shetland was added to the pawning in 1469. The Scottish kings had long desired the Northern Isles, so when the Danish king couldn't pay his daughter's dowry, his son-in-law annexed the islands in 1472.

The new rulers soon took control of all aspects of island life, including dismantling the laws and even eradicating the Norn language, which had been spoken for centuries. As the islands were no longer under the protection of the king of Denmark and Norway, they fell victim to raiding by Danish pirates. On the island of Unst in Shetland, no one was feared more than the 'Denschman' (the Danish Man), who raided the islands in his ship, the *Erne*. An erne was the Old Norse word for an eagle, and this ship lived up to its namesake. It was fast and showed no mercy to its victims. The ship was dark in colour and its lines were known to all in Unst. When the *Erne* was sighted the people fled in terror and hid in the hills, leaving their homes to be plundered by the Denschman and his crew.

One midsummer, the fishing fleet from Unst were at sea when a storm began to form, driving then back home to the shelter of their voes. The women were relieved to have their menfolk home and safe, but their joy soon turned to fear when they heard that the *Erne* had been sighted near the Holm of Gloup in Yell. The people fled to the hills in despair, despite the stormy weather.

At last, the *Erne* was sighted to the west of the island, between Hermaness and Windwick. The fishermen thought that it would lie behind Muckle Flugga to the north of Unst, in the shelter of its cliffs, until it was safe to lower boats to attack. But it was soon apparent that the ship was in trouble. It was very low in the water, like it had sprung a leak and the sea was pouring into it.

All who watched prayed that the ship would be taken by the sea, and that they would be free of the Denschman and his evil crew for once and for all. An old uddler, a wealthy farmer on the island, said that the Denschman was trying to beach the ship on the Ayre of Windwick, but the ship wasn't responding to the helm. It missed its target and was carried on to the Holm of Windwick, a small island, and its side suffered a terrible gash that sealed her fate. It was carried along by the sea until it struck the rocks at Flubersgerdie, and was broken into pieces.

The people were safe to return to their homes and wait out the storm. After two days, the wind dropped and it was safe to take a boat out to where the *Erne* had met its end. Soon they were finding pieces of wood, canvas and ropes floating on the sea, which they collected eagerly. Wood is a scarce commodity in the islands and a shipwreck had its own value to the islanders.

Suddenly, one of the fishermen cried, 'It's the Denschman!'

All the men looked where the man was pointing, where they saw, to their horror, that the Denschman was standing in the mouth of a cave that had been cut by the sea into the cliff face. He was waving a sword defiantly and shouting curses at them. They saw a large plank of wood in the sea below the cave, and guessed that this had been his means of reaching the safety of the cave. Panicked by the sight of him, the men turned their boats and rowed away. They discussed what they should do next. They decided that although there were six of them and they could overpower him, it would still likely cost the lives of two or three of their number.

They saw that there was an overhang in the cliff above the cave mouth, so he couldn't climb upwards. There were rocks on either side of the cave mouth just under the surface, and with the strong tide he would be torn to pieces and drowned if he tried to swim to safety. As he had no food or drink it was decided that they would leave him there to die. Their courage returned to them, and they rowed back to the cave and retrieved all the wood that floated there, to prevent their enemy from using them as a float. Then they headed for home with the news.

The next day, more boats returned to look at the Denschman, who said nothing this time. He just sat on a ledge of rock and stared at them. More boats came the following day, to gloat at the fate of their former foe, but again he showed no sign of interest. Days passed, and more boats visited the cave, which now bore the name 'The Denschman's Hadd'. A 'hadd' in Shetland is the hole or den of a wild animal, like an otter. But as the days passed, they noticed that the Denschman was not growing weaker. By rights he should have been dead of thirst or of cold by now, but he seemed to be as strong as ever. People started to whisper that he must be under the protection of the Devil himself, otherwise how could he survive for so long? The only thing that could save him was if a man was supplying him with food, but what man on Unst would do such a thing to one who had brought so much misery to the island?

After two weeks, the Denschman was as strong and defiant as ever. The women said that it was a shame on the men to leave him there, they should attack him and kill him. The men were not keen on the idea. They had seen how he swung that sword of his. But they decided that they would go the following day with a boat full of sharp stones, and they would stone the Denschman and then climb into the cave with staves and axes and finish him off.

The old uddler, being the wealthiest man on the island, had the largest boat, so it was decided that they would use it. Stones were gathered, and the men set off on the agreed morning to attack and kill the Denschman. He asked his three beautiful fair-haired daughters to pray for them, and they said that they would. The three young women stood and watched as the men headed towards the beach where the boat lay. When the men got there, the boat was gone. It hadn't sunk, or they could have easily raised it again. It hadn't drifted away either, as the sea was flowing towards the land. A murmur started to circulate among the stunned men: 'The Denschman …'

Another boat was prepared, and sailed towards the Denschman's Hadd, but the cave was found to be empty. He had been seen there on the previous evening, but now he was gone. How did he get out? No man on the island would have helped him, that was for sure.

Weeks passed, months passed, but there was still no news of the Denschman or the uddler's boat. Everyone on the island felt sure that the Denschman had taken the boat and that he was alive and well and plotting his revenge on the islanders. Then one autumn afternoon, a strange ship was sighted sailing towards the island. It had a sinisterly familiar look to it, but it couldn't be! They had seen the *Erne* smashed to pieces on the rocks. How could it be here again?

The strange ship was flying a white flag, a sign that it had come in peace. Behind the ship a boat was being towed. Some of the Unst men prepared their boats and rowed out to the ship, but they stopped when they saw a familiar sight on the deck. It was the Denschman.

He ordered them to come no further. 'Take the uddler's boat back to him. There are gifts in it for his three fair daughters. Without those fine young ladies, I would have gone through your isle with sword and flame. You owe them much, as do I.'

The men took the boat in tow and rowed back to the shore while the ship turned and sailed away. The old uddler, who was standing on the shore, examined the contents of his boat: silver tableware, golden jewellery, silk dresses, white linen, fruit, wine and grain. The old man turned to his daughters and said, 'Can you answer this riddle for me?'

The two youngest daughters fell on their knees in front of their father and begged to be forgiven. The eldest daughter, a proud and fearless woman, said in a low voice: 'We saved the Denschman. We knew the harm that he had done to us, but he possessed such a brave and bold spirit that his plight touched our hearts. To die in such a miserable hole was more than our hearts and our honour could stand. We took him baskets of food, drink and warm clothing at night when you all slept. That was why he didn't perish like an animal in a snare. Then, when we heard that you intended to attack him, we couldn't bear for him to die such a shameful death. We also knew that many of you here today would fall by his sword. Your deaths weighed heavily on our conscience as well. We took your boat and rescued him, but we made him swear that he would never harm a soul on this island again, and he agreed. He is a man of his word, as you have seen by his deeds today.'

An old woman said, 'The lass has spoken words of wisdom.'

'Aye', said one of the fishermen, 'and where would we men be without the tenderness and wisdom of the lasses?'

The old uddler felt humbled by the bravery of his daughters, and he forgave them. The Denschman kept his word, and he never brought harm to the island again. And it was said that Unst did benefit from his benevolence for many years after that.

THE SELKIE BOY OF BRECKON

Shetland

In the north of the island of Yell is a place called Breckon. Here there is a beautiful beach where white sand sparkles and glitters from sea-ground mica rock.

Once there was a beautiful young girl who lived on a croft near to this beach. All the local boys were in love with her, and it was no wonder, for she was a rare beauty indeed. But the girl had no interest in the boys and she never gave them any encouragement. They grumbled, they sulked, they called her a 'cold fish', but what did she care? She was quite happy to remain single, and was in no hurry to be tied to one of these local lads. No, she lived her life and loved her freedom, although she worked hard on the croft with her mother and father.

One day, the girl was sent down to the beach to gather a kishie (straw basket) full of shell-sand from a small geo that was just along the coast from the Sands o' Breckon. Shell-sand was an important element to have, for the roughly broken up seashells were fed as grit to the hens, to help them form their eggshells and grind up their food.

A geo is a small inlet from the sea, and this one was a good place for gathering the right size of shell-sand. Once her kishie was full, she swung it on her back and started to walk home. It was a lovely, hot summer's day, and she was starting to get drowsy. Walking along the coast, she came to another geo that cut into the land. It was filled with the same silvery sand as the beach. She sat down to watch the sun sparkle on the tops of the waves and on the glittering sand. She laid aside the kishie, to rest for a while. The gentle sound of the sea lapping on the shore and the warmth from the sun made her sleepy. Soon she lay down on the sand and drifted off.

As she slept, she had a dream. A tall, handsome man with brown hair and dark eyes was walking along the sands towards her. He sat next to her and smiled; such a warm smile, she thought. When she woke up, she picked up her kishie and headed home. Her mother was worried, for she had been away for some time, but she was happy to see her daughter home, safe and sound.

The days passed, much as they always do, with working on the croft and spinning wool. But as time went by she started to notice that strange things were happening to her. Soon it became plain to see that the girl was pregnant. Her father was furious, demanding to know who the father of the child was. The poor girl could not give him an answer, for she had never lain with a man in her life. Still, you could not escape the fact that she was indeed going to have a baby. Her father raged and her mother wept. In those far off days, it was a great disgrace to have a baby born out of wedlock, and soon the girl found herself spurned by the neighbours.

A baby boy was born at that house, but it was a strange thing to look upon. It had webs of skin between every finger and toe, and its body was covered in a soft, brown hair. This only made matters worse for the girl. Her father's heart didn't soften when he first saw his grandson, but rather became harder than ever. A lump of granite would have felt like wool compared to that man's heart.

One day, in a fit of rage, he again demanded to know who the father was, and again she had to answer that she didn't know, as she was still a maiden. The shame that her father felt, the anger and hatred that boiled inside of him, flowed over. He ordered his daughter and her child to leave the house immediately. Her mother wept even harder than before, but to no avail.

The girl and her baby were thrust out the door and she had to wander to find a shelter for them both. A small run-down hovel became their home, but she was destitute. It lay by the shore, and the cry of the seagulls and the surge of the sea were the only sounds that they could hear. The baby seemed soothed by the sound of the waves.

It was a hard life she now had, with cold and hunger as her only companions. She would cry herself to sleep at night. On one of those sorrowful nights, she had a dream. The same tall, dark man came to her and told her that he would help her in her need. If she went down to that geo where they had first met and dig in the sand, then she would find silver. He warned her that the silver was for the child, but as its mother she could have a share of it. He told her that she must not be greedy, and to take only as much as they needed at a time.

The next morning she took her baby and went back to that geo and dug in the sand. Among the silvery sands were real silver coins, as the man had said. She did as she was told and only took as much as she needed. She covered the rest up. After that she was able to support her child by digging in the sand for silver, but she never took more than was needed.

The boy grew up and spent a lot of time swimming in the sea. You see, the boy was more seal than human, and the waters were his natural element. Eventually, when he was just twelve years old, he kissed his mother goodbye and went off to a life at sea. She never saw him again. But the next time that she went down to the geo and dug in the sand, there were no longer any silver coins to be found.

She is long gone now, the poor soul, but ever since, that geo has been called the Silver Geo.

THE STOLEN BOOTS

Shetland

The island of Fetlar, like all of Shetland, is not famous for its forests. This made timber a very valuable commodity in years gone by, and beachcombers walked the shore looking for driftwood. I am sure that the same rules applied in Shetland as they did in Orkney, where if anything was washed ashore it was regarded as claimed if someone set it up on the shore, above the high-water mark. No one would dare touch it, as it was basically regarded as theft.

One day in Fetlar, long ago, the cry went up that there was wood washed ashore in the Geo of Funzie, on the east side of the island. All the able-bodied men ran to the shore, and sure enough, the geo was filled with wood. No one knew where the wood had come from, whether it was a deck cargo that had been washed overboard on a ship, or the main cargo of a ship that had been wrecked. Maybe the ship now lay in pieces, scattered over the seabed, the victim of bad weather. But there was no time to ponder where it had come from; the sea had brought it to them, and it could just as quickly take it away again.

The wood that lay on the beach was carried up and carefully stacked on the banks – the land above the shore. After the easy timber was gathered, the men had to secure the wood that was still afloat. Men had ropes tied around their waists, and they waded out to grab any passing plank or spar that they could lay their hands on. They worked hard all day, and late into the afternoon. The winter sun was now low in the sky, as they toiled in the semi-darkness.

One man seized a fine bar of teak, dragging it towards him through the waves. But as it got nearer he saw, to his horror, that it had the corpse of a man clinging to it. Now the source of the wood was a bit clearer. The man had his arms slung over the piece of wood, which had been a capstan bar, in an attempt to keep himself afloat. The bar, with the corpse draped over it, was pulled ashore and the silent men gathered around it. It was decided that the drowned sailor should be buried right away, and not left on the beach as carrion for gulls or ravens. But in those days, a dead body washed ashore was not allowed to be buried in the kirkyard. It was considered bad luck. The sea took its toll on the people who worked on it, or whose livelihood depended on it. It would claim a life, and if that victim was taken away from it, then it would seek to take its revenge upon the person who deprived it of its prey. You put your own life, or the life of a family member, at risk if you did such a thing. Also, if buried in a kirkyard, then the sea would try to flood over the burial ground in an attempt to get the corpse back. No, the kirkyard was not the place for a seaborne corpse. They were to be buried next to the coast.

The men undertook the grim task of transporting the corpse up the beach and then digging a grave for him. As there was plenty of wood, they decided to line the grave with wooden planks rather than making a coffin. There was no time for that anyway as it was starting to get dark. The bottom of the grave was lined with wood, as were the sides and ends, and then the corpse was laid inside.

One man noticed that the dead sailor was wearing a fine and expensive pair of sea boots. The soles were of wood, while the uppers were made of heavy, yet pliable, leather.

'Look at those boots!' he said. 'I'm having those! They look just my size too.'

'No!' shouted an older man. 'Have you taken leave of your senses? You can't steal from the dead. God forbid, you will bring a curse down on your head that you would long regret. No, let him lie there with his boots on his feet and not rob the poor soul.'

Planks were laid over the grave, resting on the side planks, and making as snug a resting place as the man could have wished for.

As it was now dark, the men left the solitary grave and walked to their homes, silent and thoughtful. If the wood was still in the geo the next day, then they would gather what they could.

The wind died down and the moon rose, nearly full now, and a few stars twinkled in the sky. Lights were shining in all the windows as the wet and weary men ate their supper by the fire. But one man was not enjoying his rest. It was the man who wanted the boots. He couldn't get them out of his mind, and he felt slighted by being rebuked in front of everyone. The dead sailor didn't need those boots now, but he did.

He waited until it seemed that everyone was either in bed or getting ready to go there, and then he slipped silently from his house. He headed straight for the Geo of Funzie, and right to the spot where the sailor had been buried. He dug into the grave, and soon his spade hit the top of the wooden chamber. He pulled away the planks and there before him was the corpse of the sailor. With great difficulty he managed to pull the boots from the man's feet, then he replaced the wooden planks and filled in the grave once more. No one would ever know what he had done.

The man ran home and hid the boots under some straw in the barn. He knew that if he started wearing them right away, people would guess where they came from and what he'd done. No, he would leave them hidden until the following year and then start wearing them. Everyone would have forgotten about them by then.

A few nights later, the man was back in his barn after dark, threshing corn by the light of an old lamp that burned fish oil. In Scotland they are known as cruisie lamps, but in Shetland they still have the Old Norse name, a koli lamp. It gave enough light to see by as he worked away, swinging his flail.

Suddenly, all was darkness. He cursed the draught that had put out his lamp. But then, to his surprise, he realised that there was no draught, it was a perfectly still night. He thought that it must be the wick that was at fault, so he went to the house for a new piece of linen. He twisted it into a wick, soaked it in oil, then lit it. It burned away merrily for a short time, and then went out again. Once again, he relit it, but this time he watched it. Soon, a long, white hand appeared through the doorway and started to play with the flame. The long, white fingers had dirty nails, but they seemed utterly impervious to the heat of the flame. The index finger toyed with the flame before snuffing it out between that finger and the thumb.

The man watched with horror, but curiosity drove him to look outside, to see if he could see anyone. In the waning light of the moon, he could see the figure of a man leaning against the barn wall. On seeing him, the man stepped forward so that his face was visible. It was the unmistakable, ghostly face of the drowned sailor.

'What do you want from me?' asked the trembling man.

'I want my boots,' said the ghost.

The man ran to the pile of straw where they were hidden and took them out. He brought them to the sailor's ghost, and held them out for him to take. The ghost looked at them, then looked at the man, and shook his head.

'I cannot take them. You must go to my grave and put them back on my feet again.'

The man shuddered, but he agreed. He returned to that lonely grave, dug it up once again and placed the boots back on the corpse's feet.

He was a changed man after that, serious and sombre in his attitude. But one thing was for certain, he never again stole anything from the dead. You see, they don't like that.

THE TROWS' BOAT JOURNEY

Shetland

In the Northern Isles the trows, as we call the wee folk, are mostly associated with the land. They live in mounds, change babies in their cradles and are generally bad news. But they can sometimes be generous in their dealings with people, as this story shows.

There was a crofter who was the very proud owner of a boat. This was not uncommon in Shetland, as the sea played as important a role in life as the land did. It was said that Orcadians were farmers with boats while Shetlanders were fishermen with ploughs. A boat was treated as well as any family member, well cared for and much admired. It was unthinkable that anyone would touch another man's boat.

At the end of another year the crofter pulled his boat up the beach to the boat noust, a boat-shaped scoop out of the banks, sometimes lined with stones. It sheltered the boats and protected it from the storms. The man had it shored up securely and covered and tied down with heavy stones. It would remain there until it was weather to go fishing again.

One day the crofter was out looking to his sheep when he saw down below on the beach that the boat was not as he had left it. He headed down to the shore and sure enough someone had been using his boat without asking his permission. This was regarded as almost a crime in the community. But there was no mistaking it. It was shored up differently and he could see the groove in the beach where the boat had been dragged down to the sea. He secured her in his own manner and went home, not a happy man.

He kept an eye on his boat after that, and a few days later he saw that she had been used again. He was furious, and worried. What if this shameless user was not a good mariner? What if the chancer didn't know all the rocks and coastline like he did? Would his boat be broken to pieces on a skerry? He was worried. And he was both angry and curious. He decided that the only thing that he could do was to keep watch over the boat at night.

That evening he went down to his boat and settled himself on the floor of the bow. It was too cold and windy to sit beside it, so he curled up and covered himself with an old sail, both as shelter and as concealment. Through a hole in the sailcloth, he could see what was going on and who it was who was using his boat without permission. He didn't have long to wait, for soon he heard the sound of boots crunching on the shingle of the beach, and voices. There was more than one person. Fear chilled his blood. He could deal with one man, but a gang of thieves? If he was scared at the thought of fighting more than one man, his terror only got worse as he saw the small hands that gripped the gunwale of the boat. These were no mortal men, but three trows.

They pulled the boat down to the sea effortlessly, as if it was as light as a crab shell. They leapt in and one took two oars while the two in front of him took one oar each. Then, with three *pjags* (hard strokes) of the oar, the boat landed on another shore. The three trows pulled the boat a part of the way up the beach and headed off, laughing as they went.

The crofter was now able to throw off the sail and see where he was. To his amazement, he recognised the place. He knew all the coast in that area, but this was a shore that was a long way from the beach where his boat lay. It should have taken hours to row there, yet the trows had done it in just three *pjags* of the oar. In the moonlight, he saw that there was a large cave in the cliffs, and that was where the trows were heading. He covered himself again and waited for their return.

He didn't have long to wait. Soon the three trows returned, each one carrying a keg. One of the trows went back to the cave and returned with a fourth keg. They then pushed the boat down to the sea and with three *pjags* of the oar they were back at the crofter's boat noust. They returned the boat to the noust and then they each picked up a keg, saying: 'One for me.' 'One for me.' 'One for me.'

Then one of the trows set the fourth keg down in front of the sailcloth, where the crofter was hiding, saying: 'One for the owner. One for the owner. One for the owner.'

It was clear that they knew that he was there all along. And with that, they were gone.

The crofter got up from his hiding place and examined the keg. It contained some sort of liquid, but he was in no hurry to stay where he was, and so he set off for home as fast as he could go. Once inside his house, he told his wife about his journey and was surprised to hear that he had not been away for long. Then he uncorked the keg and found, to his delight, that it contained the finest brandy he had ever tasted. Not that he had ever had the opportunity of tasting much of it before. The keg was carefully set aside for the Yuletide celebrations.

When Yule came there were people visiting and the best food was set out for them. Along with the strong home-brewed ale there were glasses of the best brandy that had ever been tasted in the island.

'Where did you get such stuff?' he was asked by the young lads of the neighbourhood.

He reluctantly told them his story of the trows' cave. They knew the place where the cave was and were determined to go and find some of this wonderful brandy for themselves.

Soon after that the young lads set off with their boat to find the magic cave. They gave three *pjags* of the oar, but the boat only moved a few feet. It was a long, weary row to that shore, but eventually they landed before the cliffs. They searched for the cave, but there was no trace of one. After a long time, they had to row all the way back again, with only aching limbs to show for it.

The crofter hoped that he might be able to stow away on the trows' next journey to the brandy cave, but they never returned. Whether it was because they had been seen, or whether the crofter's careless talk cost him the chance, his boat was never again used by the trows.

THE SELKIE'S BARGAIN

Shetland

When you think of the coast you may think of sandy beaches or a stone-strewn shore with seaweed growing on the rocks. But to an islander like me, we know that the land doesn't stop at the coastline. Out at sea there are skerries, which are a danger to ships and boats alike. These jagged reefs can remain above the water or lurk underneath at high tide, waiting for a victim. They are feared, but they can also be useful, as we shall see in this next tale.

To the west of the Shetland mainland lie the Vee Skerries, a dangerous group of rocks that have claimed many shipwrecks over the centuries. It is where seals like to gather, to bask in the warmth of the sun on a summer's day. This also attracted the men who hunted them, as their skins were valuable and their blubber was rendered down for oil to light their homes. It was rare that anyone would eat a seal, only in times of famine or poverty would anyone be driven to do such a thing.

One day, a boat full of seal hunters set off from Papa Stour to the Vee Skerries to club and skin seals. They were busy at their bloody work and had killed several seals, skinned them, and placed the skins in their boat. But the weather is very changeable in the north, and so it was that day. A storm started to rise, forcing the men to abandon their work and head back to their boat as fast as they could. One man was further away, and he didn't make it back in time. The boat had to push off from the jagged rocks or risk being smashed to pieces. The men tried to return for their companion, but it was too dangerous to land on the skerry. If they stayed out any longer the boat, with all the men, would have been lost.

Reluctantly, they had to row back to Papa Stour to save themselves, but they intended to return once the storm was over to see if their friend had survived. The man on the skerry watched in horror as the boat headed away from him. The wind was howling, and the waves were sweeping over parts of the skerries. It was only a matter of time before he would be swept into the raging sea or die of exposure. Once the boat was out of sight all hope of rescue was gone.

The abandoned man huddled down among the pointed rocks of the skerry to try to find some shelter from the biting wind. But what he saw next took away all thoughts of the fate that awaited him. With the hunters gone, the seals started to swim back to the skerries. They came to the skerry where the clubbing had been carried out, and which was still littered with the carcasses of the slaughtered seals. They hauled themselves clumsily up onto the rocks and then the man beheld a sight that few have ever seen. The seals shed their skins and stood up in human form. Beautiful people they were as well, both the men and women, graceful and slender. How unlike their sea form were the selkie folk. They walked over to where the bloody remains of the seals lay, and they set up a wail of grief. They touched the bodies tenderly, giving them a little shake as they did so.

The man watched in disbelief as the dead seals started to twitch and move. They were no longer a bloody mass of flesh and blubber but transformed into people as well. They had not been killed, only stunned by the hunters' clubs. It was like they had just been awakened from a terrible dream. Then, looking down at themselves and realising what had been done, they too started to wail and lament their fate. Their seal skins had been taken and they could no longer return to their homes in the sea. They were condemned to live on the land, a fate for which they were not suited.

The frightened man now caught the eye of one seal woman. She looked at him for a time, then looked at one of the victims, a well-built young man. It was as if she was thinking hard, yet trying to summon up the courage to act. After a time she walked over towards the man's hiding place and looked into his eyes. The look of sorrow on her face touched the man's heart. She spoke to him in a calm, clear voice.

'Man, my name is Gioga and you have taken the skin of my son, Ollavitinus. You will perish if you stay here, but I will make a bargain with you. I will take you to your island if you give me back my son's skin. Do we have a deal?'

'But how can you save me?'

'You can ride on my back, and I will carry you to your home.'

'But I won't be able to hang on to you in this sea. Let me cut holes in your skin, at the shoulder and flanks, so that I may hold on with my hands and feet.'

'I will let you do that. In return for my son's skin. It is silver and dappled with black, very beautiful. You must give it back.'

The man agreed and the selkie woman walked down to the water's edge with him, while the others cast accusing looks at their enemy. Gioga slipped on her seal skin and returned to her sea form. The man cut four holes in her skin, two at the shoulder for his hands and two in her flanks, which he slipped his feet into. The great seal then plunged into the sea and began to swim towards Papa Stour. The sea was cold, and the spray was blinding, but he was being carried home.

They landed at Akers Geo and the man hurried to the small shed where the men stored the seal skins. The boat was there, shored up and safe from the wind. He went inside and found the silvery skin dappled with black, and he ran down to the shore where Gioga was waiting for him. He gave her Ollavitinus's skin, and she slid away into the sea, carrying it.

His friends were amazed to see him back, safe and sound. But he was a changed man. He spoke out against the clubbing of seals and warned his friends not to continue their brutal work. They laughed at him and some thought that he had been driven mad by the fear of being marooned on the Vee Skerries. But one thing was sure, that man never went to the seal hunting again, for the rest of his life.

ASSIPATTLE AND THE MESTER STOORWORM

(Alternative Version)

Orkney

The story of Assipattle and the Stoorworm is well known, but there was another version, recorded on the island of Sanday by Walter Traill Dennison in the nineteenth century. In it, we find other characters, Assipattle's sister and a wicked queen, and it also has a different ending. The monster is often named 'The Muckle Mester Stoor Worm', which is a name with three elements from three languages, all meaning the same thing. 'Muckle' is Scots for large, in Orkney dialect 'mester' means large and in Old Norse 'stoor' means large. The Old Norse word 'orm' means anything serpentine, from an earthworm to a dragon. So the name could be read as 'The Big, Big, Big Serpent'.

There was once a farmer, who lived on a fine wee farm called Leegarth. It was sheltered by the surrounding hills and a fine stream ran past it, which gave them good, clean water to drink. The farmer and his wife had a large family, seven sons and one daughter. The youngest son was called Assipattle, meaning 'ash raker', because he slept by the fire and was covered with ashes. His clothes were tattered and torn, his hair tangled, and whenever he went out the ashes would blow from him, like smoke from a fire. Assipattle was given all the dirty jobs to do, like fetching peats for the fire, sweeping the floor and cleaning the hearth. He did all the jobs that his brothers thought were beneath them.

Assipattle's brothers hated him, and they kicked and abused him whenever they had the opportunity. He was regarded as stupid and lazy. His parents never intervened. They just laughed when he got a kick up the backside that sent him sprawling. But his sister was different. She was sweet and kind by nature and she loved Assipattle more than her other brothers. Assipattle did have one thing that he was good at, and that was storytelling. He would entertain his sister with stories about trolls and giants, which she loved. His brothers hated his stories, mostly because he cast himself as the hero of the piece who won out in the end.

One fine day, a horseman arrived at Leegarth with a message from the king himself. His Majesty ordered that Assipattle's sister should come to the castle and be a maidservant for his daughter and only child, the Princess Gem-de-lovely. The king had heard that the maiden of Leegarth was of a gentle and kind nature and was highly regarded, so that's why he had chosen her. There was great excitement at the house as they got everything ready for the young woman's departure. She was dressed in her finest clothes and her father made her a pair of rivlins, a type of shoes made of untanned hide. She was excited about her shoes, as she had never had a pair before. She always went barefoot.

On the appointed day, the king's messenger returned with a pony for Assipattle's sister to ride on, and she left her family to live at the castle. The family soon returned to their normal lives; all, that is, except Assipattle. He was quiet, withdrawn and sad. Now he had no one to tell his stories to, and his life was a lonely one.

One day, terrible news reached Leegarth. The Stoorworm had arrived suddenly on the coast of their country. This was no ordinary stoorworm, but the Mester Stoorworm, the biggest, baddest and most dangerous stoorworm in all the oceans of the world. He was said to be the father of all the great sea serpents that plague humanity. He was the oldest of his race, and it was said that he had been created by the Devil himself.

He had grown so big that he encircled the whole world, and when he moved, he caused tidal waves and earthquakes. His breathing was said to cause the tides to ebb and flow. He could devastate whole towns and cities, cracking open the walls of the strongest castles between the forks of his tongue and eating all those inside. His breath was poisonous, and it killed all that it touched. This worm was now on their shores, and it had started to yawn, which was a bad sign. It didn't mean that the monster was tired, it meant that it was hungry and wanted to be fed. You could feel the fear in the air, and the lamentation of the people was great.

At this time there was a mighty sorcerer who lived in the kingdom who was both revered and feared in equal measure. The king did not like him, as he didn't trust him. There was something about him that made the king uneasy. His skin crawled whenever he saw him. Now the king had to act to save his kingdom, and a great Thing was called. This was where all his most powerful supporters and warriors could offer their council on how they should act. The talking went on and on, but no solution was found.

Then the queen came to address the Thing with her advice. The queen was the king's second wife, and stepmother of the princess. She was a bold woman and overbearing in nature, but her words carried some weight. She stood up straight and started to speak.

'You are all great men and brave warriors when it is only men that you face. But here is a foe so deadly that it threatens our very existence, and against which your weapons are weak and puny by comparison. It is not by force of arms that this monster will be defeated, but by sorcery. Take council with the great sorcerer and listen to his advice. His wisdom will win where strength fails.'

The sorcerer was called, and the great question was laid before him. He said that it was a weighty subject and he would have to think it over, but he would have their answer by the following sunrise.

At dawn the next day, the sorcerer returned with his answer. In order to save the land, seven maidens would have to be fed to the Stoorworm once a week. If this plan failed, then there was only one more thing that could be done. But it was too terrible a thing to say at this moment in time. So, every Saturday morning at sunrise, seven innocent maidens were bound hand and foot and set on a rock by the shore as the Stoorworm's breakfast. It would yawn seven great yawns, flick out it's huge, forked tongue and pick up the maidens, one by one, and eat them.

One Saturday, the family from Leegarth went to watch the Stoorworm eat his terrible breakfast. The women sobbed and screamed at the sight, while the men groaned and sat with their heads in their hands. It was a terrible sight to witness, and the lamentation of the people was profound. But up stood Assipattle and cried, 'I am not afraid of this monster! I would gladly fight and kill it!'

His brothers kicked him and told him to go back home and grovel in the ashes. But he carried on saying that he would kill the Stoorworm, until his brothers were so annoyed with him that they threw stones at him.

That night, Assipattle's mother sent him to the barn to tell his brothers that their supper was ready. They were threshing sheaves, to feed the straw to the cattle, when Assipattle arrived. They grabbed him and piled straw on top of him and sat on him. He would have been suffocated had his father not caught them at their murderous deed. At the supper table, the father was scolding his sons for their behaviour, but Assipattle was unconcerned.

'You need not have come to my aid, Father, for I could fight and beat each and every one of them.'

Everyone laughed, saying, 'Why didn't you try then?'

'Well, I'm saving my strength for when I fight the Stoorworm.'

His father just shook his head. 'You'll fight the Stoorworm when I make spoons from the horns of the moon!'

Now, the cries of the people became too loud for the king to ignore any longer, and he called the Thing together once more. The sorcerer was summoned and asked what the second remedy was, for ridding the land of the Stoorworm. The sorcerer stood proud. His great grey beard hung down to his knees and his hair formed a mantel around his shoulders. He looked grave as he pronounced the doom.

'Oh, Your Majesty, I would rather die a thousand deaths than to have to tell you what you must do. It is a cruel fate that hangs over this land. To be rid of the Stoorworm for once and for always, you must sacrifice the fairest maiden in the land to the monster. You must give it your daughter, the princess Gem-de-lovely, to feast upon. After that, it will leave the land for good.'

A terrible silence fell over the room. At last, the king stood up, grave and sorrowful, and said, 'If she must die then so be it. She is the most precious thing in the world to me, but if by her death the land will be spared, then it must be done. She is my only child, and heir to the throne, but if by her sacrifice her people can live, then so be it.'

The Lawman asked if this was the will of the Thing, but no voice broke the silence. One by one they raised their hands and sealed the princess's fate.

Then the king's Kemperman (champion) stood up and said, 'Let this doom, like other beasts, have a tail. And that tail shall be that if the Stoorworm does not leave after eating the princess, then its next diet shall be the sorcerer.'

A hearty cheer broke from the throats of all those present.

Before the princess was to be sacrificed, the king asked for three weeks' grace in order to find a hero to fight and kill the monster. A proclamation was sent around the neighbouring kingdoms, offering the Princess Gem-de-lovely's hand in marriage, along with the kingdom to which she was heir, to the man who could slay the beast. Not only that, but the king's magic sword, Sickersnapper, which had been a gift from the god Odin to his ancestor, would be given as well.

The goodman of Leegarth was also at the Thing that day, and he returned home with the news that the princess was to be offered to the monster. Everyone was deeply saddened, as Gem-de-lovely was much beloved by everyone. Well, everyone except one person. Her stepmother, the queen, hated her, and she didn't grieve for the princess' impending death.

Thirty-six great champions rode into the kingdom! But, when they saw the size of the Stoorworm, twelve of them fell ill and had to be carried home, boots first. Twelve ran away back to their own country and hid. The remaining twelve skulked around the castle with their hearts in their boots. On the eve of the battle a great feast was held, but it was a joyless event. The champions ate little but drank deeply.

When they had retired to their rooms the old king was left with his Kemperman. The king stood up and opened the great chest on which he had been sitting. It was the high seat and contained all the precious things that the king held dear. From out of the chest, the king took the sword, Sickersnapper, and drew it from its scabbard. His Kemperman watched him with interest.

'Why do you take out Sickersnapper, my lord? It is four score and sixteen years tomorrow since you came into this world. You have done many mighty deeds in your time, but your day for fighting is behind you now. Let Sickersnapper lie, for you are too old to wield it now.'

'Silence!' snapped the king. 'Do you think that I, of the bloodline of Odin, would stand by and see my child devoured by that filthy worm? Do you think that I would not strike a blow to save my own flesh and blood? I tell you, and with my thumbs crossed on the edge of Sickersnapper do I swear it, that I will spill the Stoorworm's blood before he tastes the blood of one descended from Odin. Now, my trusty Kemperman, go to the coast before the dawn and prepare me a boat, with sail hoisted and bow seawards. Guard it until morning when I shall arrive. Do this last thing for me. Now, goodnight, old comrade.'

With that the king walked to the door, leaving the Kemperman with tears in his eyes. But the king's rhymer, who was lying on a bench pretending to be asleep, leapt up and sang:

Where fire burnt, is embers cold
The man that once was bright and bold
Is now frail, blunt and old
And cannot Sickersnapper wold
A dead cinder and cold ash
Can never save the bonnie lass

The king threw an ale cog at the rhymer's head, but he was too fast for him, and dodged the missile. Thus ended the feast.

Now, at Leegarth, preparations were being made for the following day's fight between the king and the Stoorworm. Assipattle lay among the ashes, but he couldn't sleep. His thoughts troubled him. He then started to listen to his parents talking as they lay in their bed. His mother was saying that they would all be off to see the princess eaten at sunrise, and her husband said that she should come with them, too. She said that she didn't want to go, as it was too far to walk and she didn't like to ride alone. Her husband said that she could ride with him on his horse, Teetgong.

Now, the horse, Teetgong, was the fastest horse in all the land. In Orkney dialect a 'teetgong' is a sudden gust of wind. This horse could run as fast as the wind, and so it was named after it. But the old woman was still not happy.

'Why on earth would you want to take an old woman like me up behind you on Teetgong? With all the grand folk that will be there to watch.'

'What?' said the old man. 'And who else on earth would I rather have behind me than my own good wife?'

'That I don't know,' said the old woman, 'but there are times that I don't think that you love me as a husband should love his wife.'

'Now, what has put that notion in your head? You know that I love you better than any woman on earth.'

'Well, it's not what you say, it's what you don't say that troubles me. For the last five years, I have asked you over and over what makes Teetgong so fast that he beats every other horse in the land. I might as well have asked a stone in the wall for all the response that I ever got.'

The old man fidgeted and thought, then he said, 'Aye, maybe you're right. It was from want of trust rather than want of love that I held my tongue. But if it makes your heart sore, I shall tell you the horse's secret. If I want Teetgong to stand still, I give him a pat on the left shoulder. If I want him to run fast, I give him two pats on the right shoulder. When I want him to run as fast as the wind, I blow through a goose's windpipe. I always keep one in the right-hand pocket of my coat, just to be handy.'

On hearing that, the old woman settled down to sleep, and soon they were both snoring. Assipattle had heard all of this, and he left his fireside and went over to his father's coat, where he found the goose's windpipe. Silently, he slipped out the door and headed to the stable. He bridled Teetgong and led him outside, but the horse reared up and snorted, as this was not his master. Assipattle gave him a pat on the left shoulder, and he stood as still as a rock. Then he climbed onto his back and gave him two pats on the right shoulder, and Teetgong raced off. But as he did this he let out a loud neigh, which woke up Assipattle's father. He recognised the sound of his horse, and he woke his sons. They all set off after Assipattle, shouting, 'Stop! Thief!' They didn't know that it was Assipattle who had stolen the horse. The father shouted as loud as he could:

Hie, hie! Ho!
Teetgong, whoa!

When Teetgong heard that order from his master, he stopped running. But Assipattle pulled out the goose's windpipe and blew through it. When Teetgong heard that sound, he ran off as fast as the wind. Assipattle could hardly breathe for the speed with which the horse ran.

As the day was just starting to dawn, Assipattle arrived in a valley, where he left Teetgong to graze. He saw a small cottage and slipped quietly inside. An old woman was lying in her bed asleep. Assipattle moved silently to the fireside. Peats were glowing in the fire. He picked up one with a pair of tongs and put it into an iron pot that was standing by the side of the fire, then he headed outside.

A boat was ready down by the shore, and in the bow sat a man who did not look too happy.

'It's a cold morning,' said Assipattle.

'I had noticed,' replied the man sarcastically. 'I have been sitting here all night until the very marrow in my bones has turned to ice.'

'Then why not come out for a run to warm yourself?' said Assipattle.

'Because if the king's Kemperman caught me out of this boat, he would half kill me.'

'Ah,' said Assipattle, 'you prefer a cold skin to a hot one. But I am going to make a little fire here to roast some limpets for my breakfast, for hunger is like to eat a hole in my stomach.'

With that, Assipattle started to dig a little hole in the ground, to make a hearth. Then he stopped and shouted, 'My stars! Gold! Gold! As sure as I am my mother's son, there is gold in this earth.'

When the guard heard this, he jumped out of the boat, ran over to where Assipattle had been digging, pushed him out of the way and started to dig in the ground himself. Assipattle took his pot with the glowing peat in it, untied the boat and pushed it out into the sea. The guard shouted at Assipattle when he found that he had been tricked, swearing that he would be banished from the kingdom.

Assipattle steered the boat towards what looked like a high mountain but was actually the Stoorworm's head. His eyes glowed like a ward fire, although some people said that the Stoorworm had but one eye. The sun was starting to rise now as Assipattle sailed onwards. He was not afraid, although the bravest warrior would have quaked with terror at the sight of the great worm. The king and his men arrived on the shore, where they saw the boat sailing away from them. The king raged, but he was too late.

The monster was so big that his body was wrapped half around the world. His huge, forked tongue was hundreds of miles long, and with it he could sweep whole towns and hills into the sea. Nearing the Stoorworm's head, Assipattle drew down the boat's sail and took to the oars, rowing nearer and nearer to the mouth. As the first light of the sun struck the Stoorworm's eyes, the creature gave a huge yawn – the first of seven great yawns before he had his breakfast. It took a long time for the monster to yawn, and there was a long time between yawns. The boat was close to the great beast's mouth when it gave its second yawn. A huge quantity of water flooded into the Stoorworm's mouth, carrying the boat with it.

Down the monster's throat went Assipattle in his boat. Down, down, deeper and deeper into the huge serpent the boat rushed. Now, you would think that it would be dark inside the Stoorworm, but the walls of his gullet glowed with a silvery phosphorescent glow, so Assipattle could see what he was doing. The water got shallower and shallower, as many passages opened up on either side. Eventually, the boat's mast stuck into the roof and the keel grounded on the bottom. Assipattle jumped out and ran with his pot and the glowing peat until at last he found the Stoorworm's liver. He took his knife and cut a hole in it. He placed the burning peat into the hole and then he blew until he thought his head would burst, until the peat flamed up and set fire to all the oil that was in the liver. As it blazed away merrily, Assipattle ran back to the boat.

The Stoorworm was feeling the heat, and the pain, and began to spew up all the water that was inside of him. The boat's mast snapped like a pin and the boat shot out of the Stoorworm's mouth on a great wave, casting it up high and dry on the land.

The king and his men had retreated to a hillside to be safe from the floods. Once the sea had subsided, the Stoorworm was a terrible sight to see. Great clouds of black smoke rose from his mouth and nose. In his dying agony, he shot out his huge, forked tongue so high into the sky that it grabbed a hold of the moon. They say that this moved the moon, but the fork of his tongue slipped over the horn of the moon, and it crashed down to earth. The Stoorworm's tongue made a huge hole in the surface of the world, which cut off the land of Denmark from Sweden and Norway. Water flowed into the hole, forming the Baltic Sea. The two great bays in it were made by the forks of the Stoorworm's tongue.

The Stoorworm curled up in his agony, and the world quaked with the force of his death throes. He reared up his terrible head high into the air, then it fell to earth with an awful crash. When he did this, several of his teeth were knocked out and fell into the sea, creating the Orkney Islands. A second time the head rose and fell, and more teeth were knocked out, creating the Shetland Islands. A third time the head rose and fell, and the teeth knocked out made the Faroe Islands. Then the Stoorworm curled up into a tight lump and died, and its body made Iceland. The flaming mountains that you see there today are caused by the Stoorworm's burning liver.

The king wept for joy. He took Assipattle in his arms and called him son, then he wrapped his own fine cloak around Assipattle's shoulders. He placed Gem-de-lovely's hand in Assipattle's and blessed the couple. He then took his great sword, Sickersnapper, and fastened it around Assipattle's waist. Assipattle rode by Princess Gem-de-lovely's side on the horse Teetgong.

As they neared the castle, Assipattle's sister ran out to meet them. She whispered something into the princess's ear, which she then repeated to the king and all who were there. It seems that the queen was in league with the sorcerer, who was her lover. They had been in the queen's bedchamber all morning, making love. The king was furious and swore to kill the sorcerer.

'No,' said Assipattle's sister, 'it is too late. They have taken the fastest horses in the stable and fled.'

'They'll ride fast if I can't catch them,' said Assipattle.

He blew through the goose's windpipe and Teetgong flew off as fast as the wind. He soon caught up with the queen and the sorcerer, who said, 'It's only some halfling brat! I'll cut his head off in a minute.'

The sorcerer felt secure, as he had cast spells around himself making his body impervious to blades. But Assipattle drew Sickersnapper, an enchanted blade, and he drove it right though the sorcerer's heart, so that it came out his back. The blood that flowed onto the ground was as black as pitch. The queen was taken away and locked up in a high tower, where she remained for the rest of her days.

Assipattle and Gem-de-lovely were married in great style, with a wedding feast that lasted for nine weeks. The king's rhymer made a long song, but only a small piece of it is now remembered:

The bonniest stone in all the land's above the king's hall door;
He came out of a filthy hole, where he lay long afore.

Assipattle became the king, with Gem-de-lovely as his queen. They ruled well and were loved by all in the kingdom. And if they are not dead, then they are living still.

HOW THE MERMAID GOT HER TAIL

Orkney

The mermaid was the first created, and her beauty and her song were beyond the words of poets to describe. The sea was her home and the shore her promenade, for you see, the mermaid had legs in the time of legends.

After a while, we humans appeared on the surface of the earth. Long, long ago there was a great queen, some say that it was Mother Eve herself. The queen enjoyed bathing in the sea, attended by her maidens. One day, after her swim, the queen left the soft caress of the water and stood on the sandy shore wrapped in a robe, when she saw and heard something that she could hardly comprehend. For there, sitting on a rock and combing her long golden hair, was the mermaid. As she combed her hair, she sang the most beautiful song ever heard.

The queen stood amazed at the sight and sound of the mermaid, but along with wonder and awe came envy and jealousy. And the mermaid was naked, which also offended the queen. She sent one of her serving maidens to her carrying a lovely gown to cover herself with. The mermaid stopped singing, looked down with disgust at the dress and said:

> I am queen of the sea, and Mermaid's my name,
> To show my fair body I don't think a shame,
> No clothes defile my skin, no dress shall I wear,
> But the fine tresses of my bonnie, bonnie hair.

The queen was outraged by this rebuff and set off angrily to her home. She and all the women of the land protested loudly that it was a sin and a shame to have this creature in the form of a woman, sitting naked on the seashore where anyone could see her. With her great beauty, what man would look on a mortal woman favourably again? And that voice! Well, wasn't that a thing to fear as well? The mermaid's beauty could only be created by sorcery and her song by enchantment.

No, something had to be done to her to ruin her looks. The women raised such a cry of anger, fear and sorrow that a doom was laid on the mermaid. After that time, instead of legs she must wear a fish's tail. But the men felt sorry for the mermaid, who had done them no harm at that time, so they added a caveat to this doom. If a man would fall in love with a mermaid, then she would have the power to remove her tail and once more walk along the seashore on her own two legs.

THE SELKIE WIFE OF WESTNESS

Orkney

On the north coast of the island of North Ronaldsay is a headland called Westness. Just off the shore, across the bay, lies a dangerous reef called Seal Skerry. Today you can see the tall lighthouse that stands

near to that spot. It was built in 1852 and at 130 feet high is the
tallest shore-built lighthouse in Scotland. It was originally planned
to be erected on Seal Skerry, but that idea was abandoned. But this
story happened long before the time of lighthouses.

The Goodman of Westness had no desire to take a wife and was quite vocal about his feelings. He thought he would be better off on his own, and despite his being a handsome young man the local lasses agreed that he was a hopeless case. They laughed at him and called him names, but this only went to strengthen his views about being better off alone.

One day everything changed for Westness. He was down on the shore when he heard the sound of laughter and people having fun splashing around in the water. He was naturally a cautious man so he kept out of sight of the strangers, but he saw a group of young people cavorting around on the shore. Next to them was a shallow pool, and beyond that lay a pile of seal skins. He knew that these were selkie folk, who had taken off their seal skins and adopted their human form. A strange notion took hold of the man's mind, and he ran towards the seal skins as fast as he could. The selkie folk saw him coming and dashed towards their skins. Pulling them on, they were soon back in the sea as seals. But Westness managed to outrun one of their number and snatched up a fine skin.

As Westness turned to walk home, carrying the skin under his arm, he heard the sound of sobbing coming from behind him. He turned and saw the most beautiful young woman following him. Her hair and eyes were dark brown, and her face was so beautiful! Westness had never seen such beauty before in his life, and feelings started to stir within him. Such fires raged through his veins, through his very soul. He wanted this girl for his own, and he was determined to have her.

The tears flowed down the selkie woman's cheeks as she sobbed. She looked on him with large, pleading eyes, and said, 'Oh, good man, please give me back my skin. Without it I am lost. I cannot go back home to my own people without it. I will never see the ones that I love most without my skin. Have pity on me and give me back my skin.'

But Westness refused her pleas. He turned around and walked home. He knew that as long as he possessed her skin, he possessed her. She would have to live with him and be his wife. What else could she do? She was doomed to follow him back to his home, to sit by his fireside and to have his children. Seven bairns she bore to him, four boys and three girls, and no mother ever loved her children more.

But there was a great sadness on her. She would often slip away and sit by the shore. As she stared longingly at the waves, a large selkie's head would break the surface of the sea and gaze at her. Then the tears would roll down her lovely face once again.

Back home, she was always searching. Day and night, openly or in secret, she would hunt for the precious skin that had been stolen from her. One day, she was left at home while her husband and their three eldest sons went to the fishing. She sent the other children off to the shore to play, but her youngest daughter stayed at home with her. The bairn had cut her foot and the wound had become poisoned, so she sat there with her foot propped up on a stool. Meanwhile, her mother was pretending to tidy up the house, but in reality she was searching for her skin.

The little girl watched her for a while then said, 'What are you looking for, Mammy?'

'Oh, don't tell anyone, but I'm looking for a bonnie skin to make you a pair of shoes with. It will help to heal your foot.'

The girl smiled. 'I know where there's a bonnie skin. One day, when Daddy thought I was asleep in the bed, he took a bonnie skin down from the wall-top above the bed. He looked at it for a short time, and then he put it back again.'

The selkie woman froze when she heard those words, then she hurried to the box-bed and ran her hand along the top of the wall. Sure enough, her hand touched the skin and she recognised the feel of it. She felt it deep within herself. It was, after all, a part of her. She pulled it down and stared at it for a moment, then she kissed her child goodbye and ran out of the house.

When she reached the shore, which was next to the house, she pulled on her skin and took her former shape as a seal. The waves washed over her, and it felt good. The next thing she knew, a large bull seal was next to her, nuzzling her lovingly. At the same moment, a boat rounded the headland. It was Westness and their three eldest boys. She swam towards it, and lifted the skin from her face, saying:

Good man of Westness,
Farewell to thee!
I liked you well,
You were good to me.
But I loved better my man of the sea.

And with those words she pulled the skin back over her face and dived down into the depths of the sea, never to be seen again.

THE NUCKELAVEE

Orkney

Of all the supernatural creatures that roamed the coastline of Orkney, none was more feared than the Nuckelavee. It was a creature like a man riding on a horse, although some said that horse and rider were one and the same. It hated humanity and would kill anyone who was unlucky enough to cross its path. Its breath was deadly and could blight crops and kill both people and animals. It was even said to cause droughts, as it has a great fear of fresh water. The horrible appearance of the creature is given in the following tale.

One night a man called Tammas, who lived on the island of Sanday, was heading for home. The light was fading as he walked along the shoreline. In this area there was a freshwater loch on one side, and the sea was on the other. On he went, humming a wee tune to himself to keep his spirits up. He was not comfortable being out so late, and with darkness falling.

Suddenly, in the distance, Tammas could see a shape moving. It was coming towards him. He stood rooted to the spot in terror. He had no idea what he was seeing, but he had a feeling that it was not pleasant. Now, Tammas knew that he had no option but to go forwards and meet this thing. He was hemmed in by water on both sides and to turn and run was a bad idea. He had always been told not to turn his back on an evil creature. This was sure to spell your death.

Tammas's heart was beating in his chest like a drum as he slowly walked towards his fate. The creature also advanced slowly, each one sizing up the other. As he drew nearer he saw to his horror that this was the most terrible, awful and evil creature known to humanity. He was gazing at the Nuckelavee.

Now the lower half of the creature's body was like a horse, but with flappers around its legs, like fins. It had a mouth as wide as a whale's and its breath came out like clouds of steam from a boiling kettle. It had only one eye in the centre of its head and that eye glowed red like a burning coal.

On its back or, as it seemed to Tammas, growing out of its back was a rider even more terrible than its steed. Its head seemed too big for its body, a huge lump that measured about a yard in diameter. Its thin neck seemed incapable of supporting such a weight and the head lolled around from one side to the other. Its long arms almost reached the ground and its hands were as big as shovels. It seemed to have no legs at all; it was attached to the horse like a limpet to a rock.

But the most terrible thing of all, the most disgusting feature about the Nuckelavee, was its skin. It didn't have any! The whole body of both horse and rider was red, raw meat that glistened in the light of the rising moon. Every muscle could be seen, flexing and relaxing. Tammas could see its white sinews twist and stretch as the creature moved, and those sinews were as thick as a horse's tether. But the most repulsive thing of all to Tammas was the black blood of the monster flowing through its yellow veins. The whole thing was a nightmare, and here it was standing in front of him, looking at him with malice.

Tammas started to walk slowly towards the loch, though he didn't know why. The Nuckelavee kept pace with him as it also headed towards the loch. He never took his eyes off the creature, for he knew that he could not outrun it, and if he was to die then he would rather face his killer. Suddenly his brain remembered what his body already knew. The Nuckelavee has a great hatred and fear of fresh water. He moved nearer to the loch as the monster crept nearer to him.

Now the horse's head was right in front of the terrified man. Its mouth yawned like a bottomless pit and Tammas could feel its hot breath burn his face. He saw the white sinews twist as the creature swung back one of its long arms to seize him. Tammas took a jump towards the loch, landing in the shallow water. As he did so, some of the fresh water was splashed onto the flappers around the horse's legs. The Nuckelavee roared with pain. The horse shied away, causing the rider to miss Tammas, who felt the wind from the creature's great hand as it swept past him.

Tammas saw his chance, as the fresh water burned the horse's front legs like acid. He raced for his life towards a small stream that ran from the loch to the sea. He knew that if he could cross flowing water the Nuckelavee could not follow him. No evil can cross running water.

But the Nuckelavee had recovered enough to give chase, and now it was angry. Its bellowing was like the roar of the sea as the creature got nearer. Tammas ran for all he was worth until the stream was just in front of him. In one last desperate attempt to seize its prey, the Nuckelavee swung its great arms again, but it was too slow and could only grab the bonnet from off of Tammas's head. Tammas jumped across the stream, safe and sound and out of reach of the Nuckelavee. The creature roared with rage as it tore at the bonnet, but it could not cross that stream to get him. Tammas was safe, but he never ventured to walk the shore at night ever again.

THE SELKIE THAT DIDN'T FORGET

Orkney

A long, long time ago there lived a young man called Magnus Muir on the island of Sanday, although he was always known as Mansie. Now, one day Mansie was gathering limpets for bait from the rocks along the shore on the west side of Hacksness when he heard a strange sound. It sounded like a person groaning with pain, but then came a roar like a dying cow. The terrible cries died away and became a light groan, like someone who was exhausted after great exertion.

Mansie saw that there was a selkie (seal) floating upright in the water, staring into a small geo – an inlet from the sea. The selkie, who was a bull seal judging by the size of it, never took his eyes off that spot. Curiosity got the better of Mansie. He decided to go for a closer look. Crossing a large shelf of sloping rocks, he could now see into the geo. There was a mother seal giving birth to her pups. He felt a pity for her as she laboured in pain, but soon two fine, white pups lay on the rocks beside her. The mother cleaned them up and in no time they were sucking at her teats.

Now Mansie had an idea. The seal pups had fur that was pure white, and wouldn't that make him a fine waistcoat? He ran down to where they lay. The mother dived from the rock into the sea, but the pups couldn't go into the sea until they had moulted their white coat. They remained where they were. Mansie picked them up and started to walk away.

The mother seal thrashed the water, crying piteously for her pups. She rolled over and over in the sea, beating herself with her fore flippers. The male seal was also in distress, but he remained out at sea, out of reach. Mansie looked around and saw the mother selkie pull herself back onto the rock. She stared into his eyes, and her look was like that of a human mother who had just had her baby stolen from her. Mansie turned to go, but the selkie's groan of despair touched his heart. He turned again and saw her lying on the rock once more. He swore that there were tears brimming in her eyes. He looked down at the two pups who were trying to suckle his jacket, and his heart melted. He walked back to the rock and set the two pups down in front of their despairing mother. Her joy knew no bounds as she gathered her pups up in her front flippers and, it seemed to Mansie, hugged them. The mother selkie looked him straight in the eyes. The look she gave him was one of gratitude and thankfulness. Mansie sighed to himself and then left them to their reunion.

The years went by. Mansie married a fine woman, and the two were blessed with children. These children grew up and had families of their own, leaving Mansie and his wife on their own again. They left Sanday and went to live on the neighbouring island of Eday, making their home on the west side.

One day, Mansie went to fish for sillock (small coal fish), to get a fry-up for their dinner. There was a good fishing spot that Mansie knew well, an isolated rock that lay off the coast. It was submerged at high water, but you could walk out to it easily at low tide. Mansie took a cubbie with him, a basket made of twisted straw, to carry home his catch. He took up position on the rock and cast the line with its baited hooks into the sea. Nothing happened at first, but Mansie was a patient man and he waited. Suddenly a large shoal of the little fish arrived with the turn of the tide. They went for the bait hungrily, and soon Mansie was hauling up fish after fish. He filled his cubbie and his heart soared. There would be plenty of fresh fish to enjoy now, and the rest would be hung above the fire to dry for another day.

The fish kept biting and Mansie packed his cubbie until it couldn't take any more. With a smile of satisfaction, he wound the line around his waist and secured it in place with one of the fish hooks. But when he turned to go, he was met with a sight that made his blood run cold. In his enthusiasm for fishing he had lost track of time … and of the tide. The sea had been flowing, and now his way back – the shore – was many feet under water. His solitary rock was surrounded by the sea, and Mansie couldn't swim. No one did in those days. How was he going to get home?

Mansie shouted for help, but his fishing place was well away from any houses and there was no one to hear him. He cried louder, but still no response. The water rose higher and higher until it covered the rock. He shouted as loud as he could, but with no success. The water continued to rise, first to his knees, then to his waist. He cried and cried, but the only reply was the call of the seagulls. The water rose up to his chest, then to his neck. Desperately, Mansie carried on shouting for help, but still no one heard. The water was starting to ripple into his mouth as his voice grew fainter and fainter. He was hoarse with calling and he could feel the sea swell lifting him from the rock.

'So, this is it,' he thought. 'My end has come at last.'

Suddenly, something grabbed the back collar of his jacket roughly and swept him off his feet. He felt himself being pushed through the sea towards the shore until his feet felt the rocks beneath him. Soon he was able to wade to the land. He turned to see who it was that had saved him, but all he saw was a large selkie swimming back towards the fishing rock. It dived down but soon surfaced again, carrying his cubbie of fish in its mouth. It swam up to the shore and Mansie waded out to retrieve his cubbie of fish.

The seal looked up at Mansie, and as their eyes met he realised that he had seen that look before. It was the same grateful look that the mother selkie had given him forty years before at Hacksness in Sandy. There was no mistaking it. He said later that he would have recognised that mother selkie from among a thousand. The look that she gave him seemed to say, 'One good turn deserves another.'

Mansie laughed out loud in relief and delight and said, in a hoarse voice, 'God bless the selkie that didn't forget!'

WESTERN ISLES

THE BLUE MEN OF THE MINCH

Lewis

The stretch of water that separates the northern Outer Hebrides from the Scottish Highlands is called the Minch and is home to a race of supernatural creatures not found anywhere else. The Blue Men, called *na fir ghorma* in Gaelic, haunt the area, looking for boats to sink and sailors to drown. They are sometimes seen lying sleeping on the surface of the sea or just under it during calm weather and they can raise storms that will wreck boats. The Blue Men are about the same size as a human. They swim after a boat and grab at its keel with their thin, blue hands. They will hold it fast, preventing it from moving. They will then give two lines of poetry, which the boat's skipper must complete with his own lines. If the poetic skills of the skipper are thought worthy, the chief of the Blue Men will release the boat from their grasp. If the poetry falls short of the mark, then the boat and its crew will be dragged down to the bottom of the sea.

One such encounter between the Blue Men and the skipper of a ship was recorded by Donald Alexander Mackenzie. The ship was stopped and would not move. The chief of the Blue Men then began the contest:

Chief of the Blue Men:
'Man of the black cap, what do you say
As your proud ship cleaves the brine.'

Skipper:
'My speedy ship takes the shortest way,
And I'll follow you line by line.'

Chief of the Blue Men:
'My men are eager, my men are ready
To drag you below the waves.'

Skipper:
'My ship is ready, my ship is steady,
If it sank it would wreck your caves.'

The chief of the Blue Men was happy with the boldness and eloquence of the skipper, and the ship was released. It was believed that the Blue Men made their homes in caves under the sea, so the skipper's threat was seen as reason enough to set them free.

THE SEA COW

Pabbay

There was once a crofter who lived with his wife on the island of Pabbay. He had taken over the croft on the island some years before, and when he arrived on the island he found that there was an old cow living on his croft. It was a remarkable animal that gave the richest milk, and every year it had a fine calf. He was able to sell some, and to milk those that he kept.

But the cow was not his only source of income, for he had a grand 'black pot', as illicit stills were called. He kept it in a cave on the north-west corner of the island, where he also stashed the barrels of whisky to mature. He made a lot of money, for his whisky was the finest drop that you could taste.

One day the crofter was sitting by the fire talking to his wife, and he said, 'I think it's time that we sold the old cow.'

'Whatever for?' asked his wife. 'Isn't she a fine milker, and she still provides us with a calf every year. No, I won't have it.'

The crofter's wife was very fond of the old cow, and she wouldn't hear a word of selling it. To her, it would have been like selling her own mother.

Time passed and once again the crofter raised the old cow's fate.

'It would break my heart to sell her,' said the wife.

'Then why don't we kill her and salt the meat for winter?'

'No! I could not eat a mouthful of that lovely old cow. You leave her alone.'

Time went by, and finally the crofter was determined to kill the cow. Sadly, his wife relented. Maybe the time had come after all, and it was agreed that the cow would be killed the following day. Now in those days, the cattle were kept in one end of the house, next to where the people lived. That night the crofter and his wife were woken by the bellowing of the cattle. They got up to see what the matter was but found that their stock were all gone. Not a single cow was left in the byre; they had all broken their bands and disappeared. The next day they searched the island, but there was not a trace of a cow.

Later, the crofter went to the neighbouring island of Barra to buy more cattle, and he asked around the old folk to see if they could shed any light on what had happened. One old man claimed that he knew the history of the cow.

There was once a great bull that came out of the sea and mated with a cow. The crofter's cow was descended from the calf that was fathered by that sea bull. When the crofter's cow heard them planning to kill it the next day, she bellowed to the others to break their bands and to return to the sea with her, which is what happened. Sea cattle are the finest that you can get, but if you try to kill one, then they will go, taking their offspring with them. You must never mistreat or kill a sea cow.

The crofter went home with his cattle, but his luck changed from that time forward. Soon after, the excise man caught him at his black pot in the cave, along with his barrels of maturing whisky. A sledgehammer was taken to the still and to the barrels, and that fine drop of whisky flowed down the beach and into the sea.

THE SELKIE WIFE OF GLENDALE

Isle of Skye

There was once a young fisherman who lived by the shore of Loch Pooltiel at Glendale in the Isle of Skye. He was a hard-working man with his own boat, but he lived alone and had no one to help him in his toil. You see, when he was born the Devil had laid his hand upon the boy's face and left his mark on him, from brow to chin. This red blaze marked him out as being a man of ill luck, so no man would crew in his boat. He was also not allowed to set foot in any other boat on the island. Superstition was strong, and despite his gentle, kind nature he could never find a girl who would be seen with him. So he lived alone, away from others. Away from hurt and suspicion and the cruel name-calling that he had received in his childhood. Although he worked hard, he never had enough to keep body and soul together. Life was hard. Life was lonely.

One day, when he was down on the shore gathering shellfish for bait, he saw a beautiful young woman sitting on the rocks. She was as naked as the day she was born, which was a shock to the shy young man. He saw that behind her was lying an empty seal skin. He knew now what she was. She was a selkie woman who had shed her skin and taken her human form. A feeling so strong gripped him. He was intoxicated with her beauty and he longed to have her. Although he knew that it was wrong, he slowly crept towards her unseen and snatched her skin.

The selkie woman saw him too late to save her seal skin, but she begged and pleaded with him to give it back. He refused. He told her of his lonely life there by the shore, working on his own and with no one to talk to, no one to love and care for. He told her why he was so isolated, and showed her the Devil's finger marks on his face. She listened silently, moved by pity. At last she made him a deal. She would come and live with him and keep him company and do some work around the house and help with the fishing, as long as he promised to treat her with kindness. He agreed, happily.

The real reason that the selkie woman stayed with him was because he had her skin and she couldn't return to the sea without it. She always hoped that one day she would find where he had hidden her skin and would be able to return to her home among the waves. But as time passed, so did her feelings towards him change. She saw what a good man he was, and she loved him. He loved her better than he loved his own life. She was his life. His love for her grew so strong that the guilt that he felt from holding her there against her will grew too much to bear. He offered to give her back her skin, but to his surprise, she refused. She knew that if she had her skin, she would have to return to the sea. But she didn't want to leave him.

The years flew by and they had three bairns: two sons, and the youngest was a girl called Eilidh. There were no bairns who were loved more than these three. For fifteen years they lived and loved together and the bairns were growing up.

One day, Eilidh came running to her mother carrying a seal skin that she had just found hidden among her father's fishing nets. Her mother stared at her long-lost skin with a mixed feeling of joy and sorrow. She knew this meant the end for her happy family, and the tears rolled down her cheek. She took the skin and set it aside. Nothing would be done in haste.

That evening she told her husband what had happened and that she now had her skin back. She said through the tears that the bairns were growing up, and they didn't need her like they used to. She longed to see her selkie family and friends back in the sea. She could not deny what she was any longer, and had to return. He wept too, but said that he would never stop her from doing what she had to. She was free to leave with his love and blessings.

It was a tearful family who stood by the rocks on the shore and said goodbye to the woman who was their wife and mother. She told her husband that if the time came when the bairns had gone and had no more need of him, and the loneliness was too much to bear, then he was to come back to the rocks where he had first found her and call her name. She would come for him and take him to her home in the sea. She hugged them all and swore her undying love before donning her seal skin and swimming away from them.

The fisherman was a devoted father and cared for his children as best as he could. Five years went by and the two sons left, one after the other. Tragedy followed not long after that. Both the boys died; I know not how. The fisherman was left alone with just his little girl, Eilidh, who was the apple of his eye. She had dark hair and dark eyes, just like her mother. In fact, she was the very image of her. But one day she too left for a job in a far-off town. Now he was all alone, and sadness was his only companion.

The days passed, one very much like another, and the fisherman grew more and more melancholy as he sat in his chair, staring into the fire. He no longer fished; he didn't have the heart to do anything. The loneliness was eating him up from the inside out.

One day, he left his house and walked down to the sea. He found himself at the rocks where he had first met his selkie wife. Then he remembered her words to him when she had left. He called her name. After a short time, a seal's head broke the surface of the water and swam towards the shore. The skin was shed and there stood his beautiful wife. She asked him if he wanted to join her in the sea, and he said that he did. She gave him a seal skin, and the two swam away to begin a new life.

The fisherman, who was now a seal, swam all over the islands with his wife. She showed him all the wonders that lay beneath the sea, and their life was full of happiness once more. But one day word came to them that their wee girl, Eilidh, had returned to the island. She was now married and had gone back to the house where she was born with her husband. What's more, she was expecting a baby. After a while, the news came that a child had been born in that lonely house by the shore. It was the first one to come into the world there since Eilidh herself.

One day, soon after the birth, the fisherman said to his wife that he wished beyond everything else to see his grandchild. His wife sighed and said that if that was his wish, she would go with him. But it would come at a cost. It would mean their death. He thought for a short time and said that it was a price he was willing to pay. That night, two seals left the soft caress of the sea and clambered up onto the shore. Their skins were shed and both mother and father walked to the door of their old home, opened it, and stepped inside.

Eilidh was overjoyed to see her parents once more and many tears of happiness were shed. She proudly showed them her son, lying in his wooden cradle. The fisherman picked up his grandson and cradled him close to his heart, then he handed him over to his grandmother. She took him carefully and gently kissed him before handing him back to his mother. They had brought a gift for him: two large, perfectly round pearls, which they placed on his pillow. With many hugs and farewells, they left the house for the last time. Their wish had been fulfilled.

The next morning the bodies of two dead seals were found lying on the beach. They were those of a male and a female seal, lying side by side, and with their flippers entwined.

THE MACLEODS OF RAASAY AND THE WITCHES OF SKYE

Raasay

In all the islands around Scotland, the fear of witches who could control the winds and seas was a common theme in folk tales. My native Orkney had a bad reputation with sailors as the abode of many witches. The Western Isles were no exception, as we will see here.

Iain Garbh MacLeod, one of the MacLeods of Raasay, had incurred the wrath of the witches of Skye. He knew them all and was always harsh in his rulings against them if any of them ended up in trouble with the law. It reached a point where the witches gathered together to plan his death. One day they gathered on the shore by the Narrows of Raasay to watch out for MacLeod's galley sailing between his island home and Portree. When the ship was far enough from land, the selected witches transformed themselves into huge cats and raced across the sea towards the ship. They all gathered at the stern of the vessel, and the weight of them made the ship capsize. MacLeod and all his men were drowned, but the cats swam back to Skye, where they took their human forms once more and celebrated their deed.

The death of Iain Garbh MacLeod seems to be based on a real event, which later was imbued with folkloric elements. An account from the year 1671 says that Iain Garbh was invited to Lewis by the Earl of Seaforth, to be a witness at the christening of his child. A great feast was held, and when MacLeod reached the shore he carried on the drinking with his crew. When they left in their birlinn (galley) they were all the worse for wear with the drink. On their voyage home a gale was blowing from the north and the drunken and inexperienced crew could not handle the ship, which capsized and sank.

Iain Garbh and sixteen of his kinsmen drowned, along with the crew. Pieces of the wrecked ship and two dead greyhounds were washed ashore, but no bodies were recovered. It was said that one of the men on board, Alexander MacLeod of Lewis, had heard a voice the night before warning him not to sail to Raasay, as the ship would sink and there would be no survivors. His loyalty to his kinsman saw him ignore the warning, and sail to his doom.

Legends started to grow around the drowning of Iain Garbh. It was said that during the voyage across the Minch, a raven was seen to circle the mast of the ship, before landing on the gunwale.

Iain Garbh knew that this was a witch in disguise, and he took his dirk and thrust it at the bird, but he missed. Such was his strength that he broke the side of the ship, which rapidly took in water and sank. The witch had been hired by Iain's stepmother, who wanted him dead so that her own children would inherit his estate.

Another legend says that the sinking was the work of a witch on Skye. Iain Garbh had a rival, Donald Gorm of Sleat. Gorm went to see a witch and promised her a piece of land at Trotternish, if she would carry out his instructions. The witch's name was Morag. She withdrew to her fireside for several hours to meditate over her plan of action. Eventually, she called to her daughter to fetch her the tub from the byre and water from the well. The water was poured into the tub, and the witch placed an eggshell on the water, where it floated. She then took herself to the high ground, where she could see Iain Garbh's birlinn when it arrived. For three days and three nights she watched for the ship to sail into view.

At noon on the fourth day, the witch saw the birlinn sailing on a smooth sea. She rushed home as fast as she could manage and told her daughter to stir the tub of water. It was noticed by the people on the shore that a sudden squall blew up out of nowhere, and the ship was in peril. It was swept around and was soon overwhelmed by the rough sea and sank, taking with it all on board. It was said that every year on the anniversary of the death of Iain Garbh, the flowing tide is always rough at the very spot where his ship sank.

Morag, the witch of Skye, never got to enjoy her reward for killing Iain Garbh. She and Donald Gorm of Sleat fell out over something, and her body was found washed up on the shore of Raasay. She had been drowned in the same seas as Iain Garbh MacLeod.

THE CRUEL SKIPPER

Grimsay

There was an old woman's house on Grimsay where people liked to gather in the evenings for singing and storytelling. One night, a boy came into the old woman's house, where a good number of people had already gathered. The boy asked the old woman why the neighbouring house was all lit up, with lights in both windows.

The old woman smiled at him and said, 'Do you really want to know? Well, I'll tell you then. There is a wife for you being born in that house this very night.'

The people who had gathered laughed loudly and teased him about his baby bride. But the boy was not a lad of good character, and he resented it. He had a very high opinion of himself, and instead of just laughing it off, he burned inside with anger. How dare they make a fool out of him, and how dare that baby make him the butt of the joke.

But some of the people who heard this knew that it was no idle banter, for the old woman was known to have the second sight. This was no joke, but a prophecy that was sure to come true.

A few years later, the boy went off to sea to seek his fortune. He was not an easy person to get on with, and was not popular with his crewmates, but he danced attendance on the officers and soon rose through the ranks. He also ingratiated himself with the shipowners and was soon given the charge of a ship. He returned to Grimsay as the skipper of a small vessel, and he strutted around like a bantam cock.

One day he saw a very pretty little girl, and he asked who it was.

'Why, don't you recognise your own wife?' someone said, and everyone around burst out laughing.

It was that baby that he hated so much. Now, instead of just laughing it off he took deep offence, and the anger and spite inside of him burned brighter than ever. He hated that little girl who had made him the butt of jokes – even yet, years after. He should be respected for being a skipper and not ridiculed. He devised an evil plan, which was more to his nature.

He sought out the girl's parents and said to them, 'I am the skipper of a ship now, and I earn good money. Let me take your little girl with me and I will have her educated at my own expense. I have family that she can stay with while I am at sea, so she will be well looked after.'

The girl's parents were poor and there was no way that they could ever afford to have their daughter educated, so they agreed. The little girl was provided with the best that they could offer, and they kissed her goodbye. The skipper smiled a cold smile and assured them that their little girl would have nothing more to worry about. They sailed away on the tide.

When they were well out to sea, the skipper ordered the ship to stop and a boat to be lowered. The crew obeyed, but they didn't know what was happening. The cruel skipper put a little food and water into the boat and then called for the little girl to be placed on board. The skipper and a couple of the crew rowed to a tiny skerry that just broke the surface of the sea. He ordered his man to put the girl there with the meagre amount of food and water, and then row back to the ship. The men were horrified and refused to be a party to this shameful and sinful deed, but the skipper was in control, and they eventually obeyed his command. The girl was left on the skerry where she remained, marooned. It was known that the sea covered that skerry at high tide, so she would not have many hours left to live. The ship sailed away, leaving the girl to her awful fate.

Years passed and the cruel skipper had quite forgotten about the girl that he had murdered. His conscience was clear and didn't trouble him. He sailed around the world, from port to port, until one day he found himself in a new country, one he had never visited before. He unloaded his cargo and waited for a new one to be loaded onto his ship. He met some of the local skippers and one of them invited him to dine with him that evening. The cruel skipper happily agreed, and he arrived that evening at the time stated. When he entered the drawing room, he saw the most beautiful young woman that he had ever seen in his life. He was captivated by her grace and demeanour, and it was all that he could do not to stare at her constantly. He took every opportunity to talk to her, and she told him about herself, but not too much. He was consumed with desire, which he thought must be love. This was one emotion that he had never experienced.

On the eve of his departure, he asked the foreign skipper if he could marry his beautiful daughter when he returned to that port in a few months' time. The man agreed, and the marriage was arranged. He was a happy man when he landed back in that port, and he hurried to see his future bride. She was even more beautiful than he remembered. The wedding day dawned. The cruel skipper dressed in his finest silks and walked to the church with a spring in his step.

When the bride arrived, he had to stifle a gasp as she glided to his side, the very picture of loveliness. The minister conducted the ceremony and the two were pronounced husband and wife. But when he tried to kiss his bride, she said 'NO!' in a loud voice.

Turning to the congregation, she said, 'This man who says that he loves me so much once tried to kill me when I was just a young child. He abandoned me on a skerry in the sea, which he knew would be covered at high tide. I watched as his ship sailed away, leaving me to die a lonely and miserable death. But I was lucky, for another ship saw me and sent a boat to rescue me. This man that you thought was my father was the skipper of that ship and he took me home to his wife to care for. They treated me with love, and their love was returned, so that I consider them as my parents. You did not recognise me when you landed here, and why should you? I have grown up since we last met and you thought me long dead. Now the prophesy is fulfilled, but I will never be your wife. You see this man standing before you? I am finished with him. I have married him, but I will have nothing more to do with him.'

And saying that, she walked out of the church without looking back. The cruel skipper's reputation was in tatters. News soon spread around the seaport as to what sort of a man he was. After that, his services were not in demand.

THE SPANISH PRINCESS AND THE FAIRY CATS

Barra

In 1588 the mighty Spanish Armada was driven north before a storm, and many ships were wrecked on the shores of Scotland and Ireland. There are considerably more stories than there were wrecks, as wild claims were made and the stories were embellished with every telling. In my native Orkney, most of the inhabited islands claim an Armada wreck despite the fact that none are known. My own surname, Muir, was said to have come from a North African Moor who survived an Armada wreck on Start Point, the easternmost part of the island of Sanday. But Barra has a story that is a mix of fact, legend and fairy tale.

In September 1588, an Armada ship, damaged by battle and storm, sought shelter in Tobermory Bay. Legend had it that this ship was the *Florencia*, carrying a fortune in gold to pay the army of the Duke of Parmar. The ship was carrying a large number of soldiers, who now needed fresh water and food. The senior officers from the ship entered into negotiations with Lachlan MacLean of Duart, who provided them with what they needed in return for the services of the Spanish troops. He used them in an inter-clan war against the MacDonalds.

On 5 November, the ship suddenly exploded, with the loss of most of the men on board. The surviving fifty or so men were retained by MacLean as mercenaries, until they were finally shipped home to Spain. It must be remembered that this was before the union of the crowns or parliaments, when Scotland and England were separate countries, and not always on friendly terms.

It has been said that the explosion of the ship's magazine was carried out by an English spy. Another story on Mull was that the Spanish had refused to pay for the goods they had got from MacLean, thinking that their armed service was payment enough. MacLean had sent a relative on board to claim the outstanding debt but it was refused, and he was locked up below decks. Knowing that they were about to sail with him on board, MacLean deliberately set fire to the ship's magazine, blowing the ship, and himself, to pieces.

It was later found out that this ship was not the *Florencia*, which returned home to Spain, and that it wasn't carrying a great treasure. It was, in fact, the *San Juan de Sicilia*. The wreck has been located, though no fortune has been found.

But on Mull, they tell a very different story about the destruction of the Armada ship. You see, it all started with a dream.

In Spain there lived a young and exceedingly beautiful princess. Her long hair was black and shone like a raven's wing, and her eyes were dark and beguiling. For many nights she had the same dream. In it she embarked on a long sea voyage, and at the end of it, she met a young and handsome prince. The prince took her in his arms and kissed her, but just as he laid her down on the bed, she would wake up. Every night the same dream. Every night she woke up feeling more and more exasperated and frustrated.

Eventually, the young princess decided that she would make such a sea voyage. Maybe she would find her handsome prince at the end of it, but this time she would not wake up. She managed to gain passage on the mighty Armada galleon, despite the dangers, and set sail. The passage was long and perilous, but her heart was strong. At last, the ship anchored in Tobermory Bay, as the princess selected her finest dress and jewels.

News reached the young Lord of Duart that a Spanish ship had made anchor in the bay. This was, of course, interesting news, but only slightly interesting. But when he heard that there was a beautiful princess on board, he ordered his birlinn to be prepared for sail. It was, he said, only right that a royal visitor should be greeted properly. The young lord set sail towards the galleon, his head spinning with thoughts of the princess.

When he reached the galleon, he was astonished at the sheer size of the ship. His birlinn, which was descended from the Viking longships, was dwarfed in comparison. But Duart was an arrogant man, and he was good at pretending not to be impressed. He climbed onto the deck and greeted the captain warmly.

Inside her cabin, the princess heard strange voices on deck and her heart missed a beat. Could this be the one? Could this be the man of her dreams? She opened the door and stepped out on deck. Duart saw her standing there, so regal, so elegant, so beautiful. She saw Duart too, and she gave a small gasp of amazement, for he was indeed the man that she had seen in her dreams. The twinkle in his blue eyes spoke volumes, and the difference in their languages meant nothing. That look passing between them said more than words could ever have done. He bowed to her, and she curtsied, then he took her hand and led her to her cabin. The couple were not seen on deck again for a whole week.

But the path of true love is seldom smooth, and there was one problem that the young Lord of Duart had not mentioned to his Spanish princess. That problem was Lady Duart, his wife. She too had her spies, and she soon learned about the ravishing Spanish princess who had come on that ship. When her husband didn't return, she knew what was going on, and she was furious. She decided to put a stop to it, and she knew who could do that for her. It was the Cailleach Doiteach Muileach, the 'very dirty witch' of Mull.

The old woman said that she could destroy the ship, kill the princess, but save Lord Duart. She cast her spells and flung them against the galleon, but they just bounced off the ship and struck a passing galley that belonged to the MacDonalds, who were most annoyed and confused by the event. The spells didn't work. The Cailleach Doiteach Muileach complained that her spells were ineffective because of the huge number of silver crosses that were in the ship. So Lady Duart knew that she needed a more powerful witch than this local one. She sent word to Cailleach Suil Ghorm Mor, the 'big blue-eyed witch' of Lochaber.

When she received the message from Lady Duart, Cailleach Suil Ghorm Mor took on the form of a cormorant and flew over to Tobermory. By the edge of a moor and under the shadows of the ancient standing stones, she cast her spells. She was more powerful than the Mull witch, and she didn't cast the spells towards the ship. Instead, she summoned an army. This was not an army of men, but an army of fairy cats. Great brindled cats they were, but huge in stature, with eyes of red and ferocious teeth and claws.

The fairy cats ran to the shore and swam to the ship. The crew were on deck, preparing the ship for sail. The cats climbed up the side of the ship and attacked the crew. The terrified sailors could do nothing to withstand these unearthly creatures, and soon the deck was awash with their blood. The cats bit and scratched and tore the men to pieces.

Only one man was able to run away and hide below deck, but the cats knew where he went and they followed him. The terrified man hid himself among the barrels of gunpowder that were stowed below deck, but the cats could hear him breathing. Slowly they made their way towards him, their hair bristling as they walked. Sparks flew from their fur as they neared him, like St Elmo's Fire playing around the mast of a ship. Some of these sparks landed on some loose gunpowder and ignited it. The ship exploded with a sound louder than anyone on the island had ever heard before. All those on board were killed, even the beautiful young Spanish princess, who had sailed to search for her true love.

Well, not everyone died. There was one survivor: Lord Duart. His wife had instructed the witch to destroy the ship and kill the princess, but not to harm her husband. With the witch's enchantment protecting him, he was saved from the fate that befell his lover and all those on board the Spanish Armada galleon. Maybe he would regret that later.

THE BARRAMAN AND THE WITCHES

Barra

Donald was a fisherman who lived at Tangusdale in Barra, on a small croft. His boat had the finest crew in the island, and they went fishing from March to June. Then at the end of June and the start of July they went to Glasgow with the cured fish, fish oil, and a general cargo to sell. They would buy provisions and then return home to Barra.

One year, Donald's neighbour, an old widow woman called Mary, asked Donald, 'Can I put my cow to graze on your croft while you are away at Glasgow? I will take her away once you are back on the island.'

Donald was a kind-hearted man, and he felt sorry for the old widow woman. 'Aye, sure you can. I see no harm in it.'

So the old widow woman brought her cow over to graze, and Donald even let her stay in the house while he was away. With the old woman's thanks and praises still ringing in his ears, Donald set off to prepare his boat for the voyage to Glasgow. They set off before sunrise from Castlebay, and as there was not a breath of wind, they put out four oars. They sang as they rowed, until the evening came and a fair breeze sprung up and they hoisted their sails. They headed for the Crinan Canal, then up the Firth of Clyde to the Broomielaw in Glasgow. They soon sold all their goods and bought a few things for themselves: hemp for making fishing lines, hooks, sailing twine, linen shirts, tea, sugar, tobacco and a jar of whisky. They enjoyed themselves around the taverns until it was time to return to Barra.

They sailed one fine morning, down the Clyde, through the Crinan Canal and to the Sound of Mull. There was a fair wind blowing east-north-east, which would make a fine crossing of the Minch to Barra. Donald was feeling happy, and he called to a crewman, who was also called Donald, 'Donald, fetch the jar of whisky and we will have a wee dram.' Donald poured out a glass for all the crew and for himself. 'Here, good health to you all,' he said, raising his glass, 'and a fair journey home. We will make Barra before the sun kisses the western ocean.'

One of the crewmen asked for another dram, but Donald said, 'We'll take a wee taste once we have passed Muldonich.'

No sooner had the whisky been caressed by their kidneys than they heard the sound of waves in the distance. The sea had risen from flat calm to a storm from the west in a heartbeat. The boat had to run before the gale to a harbour on the north side of Coll. They sat there overnight until the wind went down and they felt that it was safe to continue the journey. But as soon as they reached the same spot, a gale blew in from the west and they were driven back to Coll. They tried several times, until Donald decided to put their return cargo ashore in a shed, to keep it safe.

No one had seen anything like it before. Every time Donald sailed for home, a gale would spring from nowhere and blow the boat back to Coll. The year was passing now. Harvest time came and went, the time for picking tatties went by, yet still Donald and his crew were stranded on Coll.

It was now the time for cèilidhs, and folk gathered around the fireside in houses and played music, sang and told stories. At one of the cèilidh houses, the crofter's horse came to the home to seek shelter, covered with hailstones. Donald was sitting next to the old lady of the house, and he heard her say, 'Oh, you poor dun horse, isn't the cailleach (witch) who is in Barra tonight playing havoc when you have to come home to shelter.'

Donald heard this and said, 'Mistress MacLean, I would very much like to talk to you.'

'Aye, so would I, Donald. You stay behind when the others go, and we can talk.'

So once the party broke up and the boat's crew said their goodbyes, Donald said that he would stay to talk to the old lady for a bit longer.

When they were alone the old lady said, 'Well now, Donald, you are a kind-hearted man, and you gave your grazing to that old widow woman. But she is a witch, and she is the one who is preventing you from getting home. But I know a thing or two myself, and I will help you.'

She took her distaff and a drop-spindle, and she began to twine a length of wool into a thread. She tied three knots into the thread and gave it to Donald.

'Now, Donald, if you follow my instructions, you will be home before sunrise, and before the witch is awake.'

Donald listened intently, then thanked the old lady and gathered his crew together.

'Well, lads,' he said, 'she told me to untie one knot and we would get a fair breeze. If we could stand a bit more wind in the sails, we untie the second knot. But on no account, she said, untie the third one, or we will raise a hurricane and we will never smell the shore again.'

So Donald untied the first knot. The wind was a fine breeze, and the boat was off. When they caught sight of Muldonich in the moonlight, he untied the second knot, and the wind grew stronger. Donald considered reefing the sails, but he was in a hurry to get home before the old widow witch got out of bed.

Soon they were safe and sound back in Castlebay, nearing the shore with the castle behind them. Donald's curiosity got the better of him, and he decided to see what would happen if he untied the third knot. No sooner had he done so than a huge gust of wind blew the boat onto the shore, cargo, crew and all. If he had done that at sea, the boat would have been lost.

Donald set off to his own house to confront the witch. She had just risen, and had the brass neck to say to him, 'Well, Donald, I am glad that you have come.'

'Get out of my house, you witch! By your devilry, you have kept me storm-bound in Coll since July.'

Donald then laid forth with a volley of oaths. He cursed her up hill and down dell. She left the house, taking her cow with her. She sold the cow and left the island; no one knows where she went. After that Donald had no more trouble when he took his boat to sea.

TIR-NAN-OG

Oronsay

Long, long ago, back in the mists of time, there lived a fisherman on Oronsay called Aodh, son of Aodh. His boat was made of a wooden frame covered with skin and he fished inshore, as it was not built for the open ocean. One day, he was out fishing at the turn of the season. The summer was fading, and the coolness of autumn was gaining the upper hand. Nevertheless, Aodh was out fishing in the shallows. He caught the flatfish that live on the sandy seabed and the whitefish who make their homes in the narrow channels between the small outer islands.

On that day, he had let his frail craft drift too far out to the open water, where the seals play. He decided that it was now time to head back to the shore, and he bent his back to the oars. But he had misjudged the tide, and he found it tugging at the boat, pulling it towards the west. Not only that, but the wind began to rise and that made his predicament all the worse. No matter what he did, he could not get his little boat to respond to his will.

Further and further he was being drawn away from his island, from his home, from his family.

The sun began to sink into the sea to the west as the boat drifted towards it. He was lost, he knew that. His fragile little boat could not survive the storm that was gathering. There was no longer any sign of his home island to the east; he was alone in the vastness of the ocean, and darkness was falling.

The waves grew larger and Aodh was saying his last goodbyes to all his family and friends, who he would never see again. He was waiting for death. Suddenly, he heard a familiar sound – the piping cries of the oystercatcher. A flock of these lovely black and white birds, with their orange beaks and legs, flew over his boat. There was something comforting in the 'pleep, pleep, pleep' of their little voices. A calmness fell over the sea, just under where the birds flew. They swept around and around his little boat, calming the waters around him, while the large waves raged beyond.

With the rising sun, Aodh saw in the distance a beautiful green island. His boat was heading towards it, gliding along on the surface of the sea like a swan. Soon, he found himself on a sandy beach, where he pulled his little boat of wood and hide above the high-water mark. The oystercatchers, who had accompanied him all the way, now flew inland, piping their farewells as they went.

Aodh looked around him in wonder. The air was so still that it seemed magical. A sense of fear started to gnaw away at him, as he felt sure that he had sailed beyond the edge of the world. Suddenly, he remembered what the old fishermen had told him long ago. He took out his knife and plunged it into a small hillock on the edge of the shore. This was to ensure that no evil could befall him, nor enchantment bind him. He wandered along the shore, marvelling at the wonders of the place.

In the distance he heard a sound. It was sweet and musical, entrancing and beguiling. It was the sound of singing, but such a voice he had never heard before. It was as if an angel had alighted on the earth to welcome him. He followed the sound of the voice; how could he not follow it? Soon he saw where the music was coming from. Sitting on a rock was a young maiden of uncanny beauty. Her long golden hair flowed over her milk-white shoulders and her blue eyes were like the depths of the sea.

She said to him, 'Aodh, son of Aodh, come to me now. Welcome to Tir-nan-Og, the Land of the Ever Young.'

Aodh sat at her feet, and he adored her. His love for her grew and blossomed with every beat of his heart. They held each other, kissed and felt their hearts become one.

They lived happily together for several years in contentment and blissfulness. But sometimes Aodh thought about Oronsay and his family there. He thought about them more and more, until one day he asked the maiden if he could return there for a visit.

'No,' she replied, 'that cannot be. For seven years you have lived in Tir-nan-Og, from which there is no return.'

'But I still have my boat by the shore. It is still sound and can bear us both.'

'Your boat can not go more than a span from the shore, my beloved, or it will sink into the depths of the ocean.'

But Aodh hadn't told her about the knife he had driven into the small hillock. It had broken the spell that would hold him there and he would be free to leave. He started to feel that this beautiful island was their prison, and he desired to escape. The next morning, he asked the maiden to come with him to look at his boat.

'Let's take it out to sea, just as far as that headland yonder.'

'There and no further can we go,' she said as she stepped lightly into the boat.

But once they had reached the headland, he turned his boat's prow towards the east and began to row for his life. Further and further went the little boat, free of the hold of Tir-nan-Og, the Land of the Ever Young. The maiden was now weeping bitterly in the stern of the boat, a look of confusion and fear on her sweet face. But her face was changing somehow. The flush of youth was leaving her cheeks. On and on they went until Aodh saw the familiar sight of Oronsay in the east.

He landed his boat in the bay, where he had set out from that morning seven years ago. He pulled the boat up the shore, crying out in triumph, 'Come now, best-beloved! Come with me to my own house upon the hill, where no evil spells can bind us.'

But there was no reply from the maiden. He called again, but she made no answer. A third time he called her, fear now growing in his heart. The gulls wheeled around in the sky above something lying among the rocks and seaweed, and the oystercatchers piped a lament. It was the maiden, hiding her face with her shawl. He bent down and picked her up. She was as light as a bundle of twigs. He moved aside her shawl, but he did not recognise his golden-haired maiden. Now her thin hair was white, and her youthful face was a shrunken mask of wrinkles. She wept to see how he looked at her.

In a thin, weak voice she said, 'Oh, Aodh, son of Aodh, let us return to the green isle where I can recover my youth. Without it I shall soon die.'

Aodh realised that he had acted foolishly, tricking her into coming with him. But the knife was still embedded in Tir-nan-Og. Could he find his way back there? He realised that all the old tales were true. If anyone can return from the Land of the Ever Young, then they lose not only their youth and beauty, but their happiness, too. With tears in his eyes, he carried his beloved one back to the boat, and he turned his back on Oronsay for the last time. He headed out to sea, towards the setting sun.

Did he find his way back? I don't know. But fishermen say that at times, a frail little craft of wood and hide can be seen far out to sea against the western horizon, ceaselessly searching for

Tir-nan-Og. When it is sighted they turn their boats for home, for it is the harbinger of a storm.

CORRYVRECKAN

Jura

Between the islands of Jura and Scarba lies the powerful whirlpool called Corryvreckan. Its Gaelic name is Coirebhreacain, meaning the Cauldron of the Speckled Seas, but it was also locally called the Cailleach, or hag/witch. This is because it was said that the Cailleach, who is the spirit of winter, uses it as a cauldron in which she washes her plaid. But the main legend is one based on love and falsehood.

Breakan was the son of the King of Lochlann, as the home of the Scandinavian Vikings who plundered the Western Isles was called. Prince Breakan fell in love with the daughter of one of the kings of the islands and asked her father for his daughter's hand in marriage. She was in love with Breakan too, and dearly wanted the match to be agreed. But her father remained unimpressed by the stranger, royally born though he was. He decided to be rid of this unwelcome suitor by setting him an impossible and deadly task. The whirlpool of Corryvreckan was known as the Coire (cauldron) at that time. Breakan was ordered to anchor his ship in the middle of the Coire for three days and three nights; this way he would show his courage and his love for the king's daughter. Breakan agreed, but he said that he would have to return home first before undertaking the task that had been set him.

Breakan sailed to his homeland to consult the wise men of Lochlann on how this impossible task could be performed. They consulted for a while and then called the young prince to hear their council. He must make three ropes that would act as anchor cables to hold his ship. The first was to be made of wool. The second was to be made of hemp. The third was to be made from the hair of maidens who were pure and had never lain with a man. Breakan had the rope of wool and the rope of hemp twisted, ready for the task. He called together all the maidens and explained his plight and begged them to cut off their long tresses in order for him to twist them into a magical rope that would never break. They sacrificed their hair for the love that Breakan bore for the island princess.

With the three ropes, he returned to the isles and made ready for the task. He positioned his ship in the middle of the Coire and anchored it, using the three ropes. The sea began to surge and swirl into a great whirlpool, but Breakan and his crew held tight, and here they passed a day and a night. On that first day the rope of wool broke, but the other two held. On the second day, the sea boiled around them. They held on tight as the time passed. And on that second day the rope of hemp broke at last, but the last one held firm. On the third day, the sea rose with a mighty roar, and the whirlpool churned and spun the ship around. The only anchor cable left was the one of maidens' hair. Breakan held firm in the belief that it could endure anything.

But what Breakan didn't know was that there was a weak link in the rope that his life depended upon. One of the maidens was not as pure and innocent as she claimed to be, but would not confess it publicly. On the third night, he heard a sound like a whiplash as this third rope broke. The ship was spun around and drawn into the heart of the whirlpool, where it was smashed to pieces. The only survivor was Breakan's faithful dog, who pulled his master's body onto the shore at Jura. He was buried in a small cave that bears his name, Uamh Bhreacain, the Cave of Breakan. The whirlpool now also contains his name, Coirebhreacain, the Cauldron of Breakan.

WEST COAST

THE DEVIL AND THE LAIRD
OF ARDROSSAN

Ayrshire

If you stand on the sandy shores of Ardrossan South Beach and look eastward you see the crumbling ruins of Ardrossan Castle, which belonged to the Clan Barclay. It was used by English troops during the Scottish Wars of Independence, but they were slaughtered to a man by William Wallace, whose ghost still wanders the castle ruins.

Before that event, it was the home of Sir Fergus Barclay of Ardrossan. He was an overbearing man, known as the De'il o' Ardrossan ... but not to his face. He was an accomplished horseman, and no one could compare to him when it came to feats of riding, no matter how spirited the horse. There was a reason for this, you see. Sir Fergus had a magical bridle that made any horse do exactly what he wanted. But where do you get a magical bridle? From the Devil, of course! The price of this magical bridle was his soul, which he gladly gave up for his prowess in the saddle.

As time passed, Sir Fergus Barclay started to worry about his fate, as he had no soul. He summoned up the Devil again and challenged him to perform a task that Sir Fergus would set him.

If the Devil couldn't do it, then Sir Fergus would regain his soul, but if he could, then Sir Fergus was doomed to follow him to hell straight away. The Devil, who is a gambling man and fond of a challenge, agreed to the deal.

Sir Fergus ordered him to make a rope out of sand. The Devil gathered sand from the South Beach, but no matter how hard he tried to weave it into something like a rope, it just flowed through his fingers. The Devil devised a plan. If he wet the sand, then he might be able to weave it into rope. But all that happened was that the wet lumps of sand fell to pieces. The Devil had to admit defeat, but he was not a good loser. He went to Ardrossan Castle and gave Sir Fergus back his soul, but in his rage, he kicked the castle wall on his way out and left his hoof print there in the stone for all to see.

Not long after this, Sir Fergus's son was killed in a riding accident. He grieved for his son, but his grief turned to anger as he blamed his wife for their son's death. In a fit of unbridled fury, he murdered his wife. For this crime, he had to flee across the Firth of Clyde. He went to live in Kildonan Tower on the Isle of Arran. Here he had a premonition that if he ever set foot on Irish soil, then he would die. He remained on Arran and swore never to travel to Ireland.

Sir Fergus had forgotten one thing, and that is fate can never be cheated. One day, as he was walking along the shore, he came to a place where Irish boats landed to pick up their cargoes. Instead of using stones, the Irish boats carried large turfs as ballast, throwing them onto the shore when they were finished with them. Without realising it, Sir Fergus stood on a piece of Irish soil. He died soon after. His body was sewn into a bull's hide and he was buried by the shore. That night, a terrible storm arose. The seas were mountainous, ripping into the coastline and tearing Sir Fergus's body from its resting place. It floated across the Firth of Clyde and landed on the shore below Ardrossan Castle. It was carried onto the land and buried in the nearby chapel of the castle. It is said that the ghost of Sir Fergus haunts the castle grounds.

THE MERMAID'S CURSE

Ayrshire

Just south of Girvan, along the Ayrshire coast, stands the ruins of Knockdolian Castle. It is haunted by the ghost of a lady whose sorrows keep her bound to the place. It is a tragic tale, which has been told in many ways, but this is my interpretation of it.

While Knockdolian Castle lies inland, it is near the River Stinchar, which winds its way towards the sea. Long, long ago a mermaid took to leaving her home in the sea and swimming up the river, where she found a large, black, smooth rock – a perfect place to sit and comb her long yellow hair. So the mermaid abandoned her usual haunt at the seashore, and at high tide she would swim up the river to her beloved rock. As she hauled herself up onto the rock over the years, the surface became smoother and smoother.

The mermaid only ventured up the river during the night time, if the tide was high, and then she would sit on her rock and comb her hair and sing. The silvery scales of her tail glinted and shone in the moonlight. The lord and lady of the castle were used to her singing, to the extent that it didn't disturb their sleep too much. But all this was about to change.

Lady Knockdolian became pregnant with a much looked-for heir to the castle and estate. The lord was thrilled with the news and arrangements were made to welcome a new generation of the family. The lord was delighted when his wife was delivered of a baby boy, the heir that he had so badly wanted. A nurse was engaged to take care of the baby, but it was a restless child.

It seemed quiet and contented enough during the day, but at night it began to cry. No matter what the nurse or the mother did, the child just would not stop crying. Now the household could get no peace from the constant wailing of the baby all night long.

One night, as the mother was walking up and down holding the baby and trying to comfort him, there was a short pause as the baby drew breath to scream once more. It was in that short period of silence that she heard the song of the mermaid. From the window the mermaid could be seen sitting on her black, shiny rock, singing her song. Now they knew why the baby wouldn't sleep at night; it was the song of the mermaid that disturbed him. Some say that servants were sent to plead with the mermaid to move somewhere else and to stop her singing, but this only made her sing all the louder. The mermaid was not going to be ordered around by mere humans! Lady Knockdolian was furious with the mermaid and swore that she would put a stop to her nocturnal singing.

The lady gathered some of her servants. She ordered them to fetch pickaxes and hammers, to go to the river and break up the mermaid's stone. Nothing was to be left above the water. The servants shrunk back and protested that such actions could only end up bringing misfortune to the family, as well as to them. But the lady was determined to be rid of the rock, and the servants had no power to stop her. She could have them all flung out of their homes, along with their families, should she so desire.

So, reluctantly, they went down to the River Stinchar to begin work. The 'Mermaid's Stane', as it was known, stood proud of the water, as black as pitch and as smooth as glass. The men managed to reach the rock and climb up onto its slippery top. With a sigh, one of the men swung his sledgehammer and struck the rock. More men joined in with hammers, and then they drove the points of their pickaxes into the roughened top until pieces started to break off the rock. Soon, larger pieces were being prised off the rock. It grew smaller and smaller until there was nothing left but jagged points, like a dragon's teeth.

Inside the castle the lady watched with growing satisfaction. Wouldn't the mermaid be sad that she had ever dared to annoy the Lady of Knockdolian! That evening the baby was settled snuggly into his crib and rocked to sleep. The lord and lady prepared for bed, along with the rest of the household. Outside, the mermaid swam up the river from the sea, ready for another night of singing as she combed her hair.

When she reached her seat, she saw what had been done. Just the broken and jagged remains of her beloved rock were to be seen above the waters of the River Stinchar. But instead of being sad and defeated, the mermaid was outraged, and the fury grew in her breast until she gave one huge, piercing scream that shook the castle to its very foundations. The lord and lady were shocked by that scream, but what the mermaid said next made their blood run cold. From the smashed up and shattered remains of her seat the mermaid made this curse, which the lord and lady heard as plain as day.

Ye may think on your cradle,
I'll think on my stane,
And there'll ne'er be an heir
To Knockdolian again.

With that, the mermaid left and returned to the sea. Now some say that a storm was raised by the mermaid and others say that it was the shaking of the castle caused by her scream, but soon the silence in the house became unnerving. They rushed to the baby's room, only to find that the cradle was tipped over and the baby lay underneath it, as dead as a stone. The mermaid's curse came true, as there was no heir to continue the family name after that day. On her death, Lady Knockdolian found no rest either.

Her ghost still wanders through the remains of the castle, lamenting the loss of her son and ruing the day she had the Mermaid's Stane demolished.

THE SELKIE'S REVENGE

West Highlands

Many, many years ago, there was a minister who lived in a manse near a village in the West Highlands. It was a poor area and sparsely populated, so his congregation was not big. He liked to spend his free time in his garden, but mostly he loved to fish. He used a rod with baited hooks, from the shore or from his rowing boat, but he also had a net that he set in the bay. He could go down when the tide was falling and gather up the fish that were caught in it, and he would share them among the old and needy in his congregation.

But there was one thing that made the minister's blood boil with anger, and that was the seals. His net was fragile and expensive, and it was not easy to replace. The seals would go after the fish, and tear holes in his nets to take them, or ruin the fish by taking bites out of them.

He hated the seals with a passion. He would rage to his wife about them, but she had heard it all before and just nodded quietly. The minister's wife was a kind, gentle soul who always saw the good in all people, and in all creatures. The minister and his wife had one child, a daughter called Morag, who took after her mother. She would sit and watch the seals and had no thought of wishing them any harm.

One Sunday, the minister went down to the shore to check his net as the tide was ebbing. He wanted to reach the net before the gulls made a feast of his fish and before he went to the kirk to preach his sermon. As he waded out towards the net he saw a splashing in the water. Something was caught in his net. He rushed forward to see what he had caught, but when he got to where his net was, he howled with rage. A young selkie pup had been caught in the net and was struggling to free itself. Strangely enough, the net had not been damaged and it was full of fish.

But the anger rose in the minister's breast, and he shouted out, 'You wee devil! You've come to steal my fish, have you? You haven't torn my net now, but you'll grow up to be a big seal and then you'll wreak havoc with my net. No, I'll not let you have the chance to do that.'

And with those words, he picked the baby seal up by its tail flippers and carried it over to a large rock. He swung the helpless wee creature and hit its head against the stone, killing it instantly. He then threw the lifeless body among the seaweed and turned back towards his net. Out in the sea he saw the head of a seal, watching him. He shook his fist at it in anger, and the seal disappeared beneath the waves.

The minister returned home with the fish and told his wife what he'd done.

She looked grave and said, 'My dear, you shouldn't have done such a cruel thing as that. Remember, the good Lord made all the creatures, both great and small, and the seals have as much right to the fish in the sea as you do. Maybe more so, in fact.'

The minister was unimpressed. He went to get washed and dressed, ready for the service.

Soon after that, the minister's wife took ill. The doctor was called, but the cause of her sickness was unknown. He tried everything that he could to save her, but she just pined away and died. The minister was heartbroken. So was their daughter, Morag, who was no more than four years old at the time. She missed her mummy desperately.

The minister found it hard work to look after his child alone while serving his congregation, tending the vegetable garden that provided them with food and fishing to put something on the table. He soon realised that he needed help, so he placed an advert in the local newspaper for a housekeeper. A week passed, then one evening there was a knock at the door.

The minister and his daughter were eating their dinner, but the wee girl got up and said, 'I'll get the door, Daddy.'

Standing on the doorstep was a young woman, maybe in her mid-thirties.

'Who is it?' asked the minister.

'It's a lady, Daddy.'

The minister wiped his mouth and went to see who this was. Maybe a member of his congregation, or a friendly neighbour checking to see how they were getting on. But it was neither of those. A very pretty young woman with long brown hair and dark eyes was standing there. The minister was slightly taken aback to see her, but he didn't know why.

'Can I help you?'

'Yes, I hear that you are looking for a housekeeper. I have come about the job, unless the post has been filled?'

'No, no indeed, the post has not been filled. Please, come in.'

The woman followed the minister into the dining room, where the food was still sitting on the table.

'Yes, the job is just looking after the housework and doing the cooking. But mostly it is to look after Morag, my daughter. Her mother passed away recently, and she needs someone to take care of her. But who are you? Where do you come from? I haven't seen you around here before.'

'No, I am new to the area,' said the woman, 'but I do need a job and a place to stay. My name is Selina, and I am a widow.'

Morag had been staring at the woman from the moment that she had first seen her. She smiled and edged towards her shyly. Soon she was clinging to her skirts.

'I am sorry to hear about your loss. But you can stay here in the manse. There is plenty of room, and you can eat your meals with us.'

The woman nodded and thanked the minister, who showed her to her room.

Two weeks passed and wee Morag was laughing again, for the first time since she had lost her mother. She was devoted to Selina and followed the woman around like her shadow. The two were inseparable. They spent many hours together at the beach, regardless of the weather, morning, afternoon, and evenings. Morag, who was a delicate child, seemed to be thriving on this brisk sea air, and she glowed when she returned from the shore.

At first the minister was happy with his employee. She was quiet and ate very little. He was now able to study his Bible, compose sermons and attend to his congregation without distraction. He had even started to go fishing again. Another two months passed before the minister started to get annoyed. He seldom saw his daughter now because she was always down at the sea with Selina. When she did return, all she could talk about was what Selina had said or what Selina had done. When they sat down for their meals, the two hardly touched their food, just picked at it and left the table at the first possible opportunity. The minister started to feel jealousy towards this stranger who meant so much to his daughter. He felt that he was losing her.

One day, that temper of his resurfaced and he decided that he would have to give Selina a good talking to. He called her to see him and said, 'Is it too much to ask that we can all sit down to a decent meal together? All day long you are at the beach with Morag. What do you do there all day, rain or shine?'

'Morag loves the sea, as I do, and she loves to swim. It is good for her, and we both love it very much.'

Another month passed, but things did not improve. Morag was becoming more withdrawn and quieter, always clinging to Selina. When they were at the Manse, Morag sat on Selina's lap, and they were always whispering to each other. The minister started to think that he must dispense with her services altogether, no matter how much it would upset the wee girl. But he decided that he would make one last effort. The following day he would take them out fishing in his boat.

The next day he readied the boat and had his rod ready for a day's fishing. Selina and Morag were none too talkative, as was now their custom. The small boat had three benches in it, one at the bow, one at the stern and one in the middle, where the minister sat to work the oars. The rod was lying in the bow and Morag and Selina sat in the stern. The minister was facing them as he rowed out to sea. Selina sat with her arm around Morag, and they were whispering to each other again.

The rage rose within the minister, and he shouted, 'Stop whispering, I'll not stand for it any longer! You, woman, should be grateful for all the kindness that I have shown you. I gave you a roof over your head and food to eat, although you hardly touch it. But now you repay me by trying to take my daughter away from me. I need Morag as much as you do – even more so, because she is my daughter, not yours. You're trying to take away from me the only thing in this world that I love.'

Selina fixed his gaze with a cold, hard look and said, 'Just as you did to me.'

'What do you mean? I have never done anything to you.'

'You took away the thing that I loved most in this world. You took my baby, and you smashed his head against a rock.'

Then, with her arm around Morag's shoulders, she fell backwards over the stern of the boat, taking the little girl with her.

The minister flung himself to the stern of the boat, but he could see nothing other than bubbles that rose to the surface, and then were gone. He never saw his daughter or Selina again for the rest of his lonely days.

THE DEMON CATS

West Highlands

There was once a fisherman called Murdo MacTaggart, who lived in a small village in the west of Scotland. Now, people who live on the coast and who make their living from the sea tend to be superstitious. Who can blame them? Their lives hang by a thread, and anything they believe to be helpful for protection is cherished. Some words are taboo and must not be uttered when at sea, and certain animals, and even people, are considered bad luck when met on the way to the boat.

But Murdo MacTaggart was not one of these people. He laughed at such superstitions, and scorned them. He was a hard-headed and sober-living man who saw no need for such precautions. Some thought that he was making a rod for his own back by flaunting the rules that were there to keep folk safe, but he cared not one jot!

Murdo tended to fish at night, as many fish rise to feed at that time. He would return at dawn with his catch. This meant that he could be early at the fish market to sell them. This had always worked well for Murdo, and he saw no reason to stop his nocturnal fishing trips.

One year at Halloween, Murdo left his house and headed down to his boat. His neighbours saw him and warned him that going fishing on All Hallows E'en was a foolhardy thing to do, for that was a night to stay ashore and go to the late service in the kirk.

Murdo just laughed at them and headed down to the shore where his boat and his net awaited.

But that night was not like all the other nights, as Murdo would find out to his cost, for evil was afoot along the shore. As Murdo neared the coast, there was a sudden and dramatic change in the weather. The wind rose and thunder rolled overhead, followed by the flash of lightning. In no time at all, a terrible gale was raging and Murdo had to seek shelter. He ran to a small building that the fishermen used to store their nets, fishing lines and sails. He ran inside to wait for the storm to pass, sitting on a small stool in one corner. There would be no fishing that night.

As the wind howled and the lightning flashed, Murdo was suddenly aware of another sound. It mingled with the howling wind, but was higher pitched, and the sound of it made Murdo's blood run cold. He looked out the door and saw a sight that made him cower with fright and regret not listening to his neighbours. The wailing grew louder as they approached the fishermen's hut. Twelve monstrously large black cats were heading for the door, led by an even bigger cat, whose fur was as red as fire. They stalked into the hut, and the black cats sat in a great circle around the red one.

Then the red cat spoke: 'Why are we sitting in silence? Come along! Let's raise our voices to sing a cumha for Murdo MacTaggart.'

Now, a cumha is an old Gaelic song that is sung at a funeral. The thirteen great cats started to yowl and wail together, making a noise that shook the walls of the hut. Between the noise of the storm outside, and the keening of the cats inside, poor Murdo thought that he would never survive. Eventually, the cats stopped their screeching, and they all turned their heads to stare at Murdo.

The big red one turned to him and said with a purr, 'Come along now, Murdo. You must pay for the fine cumha that the cats have sung for you.'

'Pay for it!' said Murdo. 'Why should I be paying for that? I don't need a cumha, what with me not being dead and all. Anyway, what do I have to pay for it with?'

'That I couldn't tell you,' said the red cat, 'but I know that singing gives you an appetite. You had better pay them, Murdo, for I can see the light of hunger in their eyes. Be quick about it, man!'

Murdo could see the green eyes glowing in the dark as the cats sized him up. He looked all around the hut, but he could not see anything with which he could pay for the cumha that he didn't even want. His gaze turned to the open door. On the brae that led down to the shore were a sheep and a skinny old cow, standing with their backs hunched up against the wind. They were not Murdo's to give, as they belonged to the laird, but he didn't care much about that. He pointed his finger towards the creatures and cried, 'Take the sheep as your pay.'

With that, the cats flew out the door and set on the sheep, tearing it to pieces and eating every scrap of flesh on its body. By the time they had finished there was nothing left of it but a pile of white bones, picked clean, lying in a heap. In a flash, the cats were back in the hut, sitting as before in a great circle around the red cat. It had happened so quickly that Murdo never had a chance to flee.

Then the red cat spoke again. 'Come along! Let us sing a cumha for Murdo MacTaggart.'

If the screeching and wailing of the cats had been awful to hear the first time, then the second was even worse. Poor Murdo thought that he would never live to see another day. When they had finished, they sat staring at him with their green eyes glowing.

The red cat said, 'Now, Murdo, pay us for the fine cumha that we have sung for you.'

Murdo pointed to the laird's skinny old cow and said, 'There is a cow up there on the brae. Take it as your pay.'

Once again, the cats flew out the door and fell upon the old cow. Now, it had even less flesh on it than the sheep, and the cats finished it even quicker, leaving only a pile of bones where the old cow had stood. Before Murdo could escape, they were back in their circle with the red one at the centre.

Then the great red cat spoke once more. 'Come along! Let us sing a cumha for Murdo MacTaggart.'

If the first two cumhas were terrible to hear, the third was the worst one of the lot. The screeching and wailing nearly drove Murdo mad. Once it stopped, he knew what was coming next. Knowing that the sheep and the cow were eaten, he looked around him in desperation, but there was nothing to give them for payment. Murdo thought it would soon be his bones that would be left piled on the floor. Suddenly, he saw outside the laird's great deerhound, sniffing at the piles of bones that had once been the sheep and the cow. It was a large, ragged, long-nosed and long-legged creature that could outrun the swiftest stag.

Before the red cat could speak, Murdo pointed to the hound and said, 'There's your pay.'

The cats flew out the door and ran up the brae towards the dog. He saw them coming, turned on his heels and ran away. He darted this way and that, with the cats wailing in anger behind him. Murdo saw his chance. He burst out of the hut and ran as fast as he could. There was a wood next to the brae and Murdo headed towards it, hoping that he might get home before the cats caught him.

To his horror, Murdo could hear the cats behind him. They hadn't been able to outrun the deerhound, who had got safely away. The fury burned in their breasts, and could only be soothed by the flesh and blood of Murdo MacTaggart! They searched around the trees and in the bushes, but they didn't see him.

Murdo had seen a very tall tree, which had no branches most of the way up its trunk. Murdo grabbed the tree and started to climb up it like a sailor climbing a mast until he reached the topmost branches, where he sat, looking down anxiously at the cats. He was just congratulating himself on outwitting the black cats, who were still searching for him far below, when the big red cat turned up. It looked up and saw Murdo sitting in the treetop.

'You can stop looking, for I have found Murdo MacTaggart for you. There he sits, like a bird, in the topmost branch of the tree. But we will soon get him down.'

An angry yell went up from the black cats.

Murdo thought to himself, 'You'll not get me down so easy.'

One of the great black cats started to climb the tree. Murdo drew his dirk from his belt and waited for the cat to reach him. When it did, it reached out with its claws spread, ready to seize him, but Murdo stabbed the creature in the heart. It let out a terrible yowl and fell down the tree, landing on the ground among the other cats, stone dead. A second one then climbed the tree, but Murdo stabbed that one, too. A third climbed the tree and suffered the same fate.

'Wait!' shouted the red cat. 'If we carry on like this then we will all soon be dead. No, we won't get him down that way, ill luck on him! We must come up with another plan to get him.'

The remaining great cats formed a huddle and spoke to each other in their screeching voices.

Then the red cat spoke. 'If we can't climb up and get him, let's bring the tree down with him in it, and then we will catch him.'

The cats gathered around the base of the tree. They scratched and bit at the earth until they uncovered one of the tree's great roots. They tore at it with their teeth until they chewed it right through. The tree gave a lurch to one side.

In the branches, Murdo was getting desperate. He cried out as loud as he could, 'Help me!'

At the church that lay on the other side of the wood, the priest and the congregation were just leaving from the late service.

The priest heard Murdo's cry. 'That is the cry of someone who is in great trouble. I may be needed. I must go to their aid.'

But one of the men with him said, 'It is a wild night, Father, and you should not go out in it. Wait a while, to see if you hear it again.'

The priest agreed, but he went into the church to gather the things that he might need, should the cry for help be repeated.

Meanwhile, another great root had been uncovered and bitten through. This time the tree lurched over even further. Murdo once more cried for help. Again the priest heard, and he insisted that he had to go. The man ran around, gathering a party of men from the congregation. They ran in the direction that the cry had come from.

The last big root had been uncovered and the cats tore at it wildly with their great, sharp fangs. The root snapped in two and the tree fell just as the priest and his men arrived. Murdo cried for help as the tree fell, climbing up to the highest branch, pursued by the cats.

The priest took his bottle of holy water and sprinkled it on the cats, shouting, 'Begone, Satan! Begone, and take your demons from hell with you. I bid you to leave this man's body and soul unharmed.'

The big red cat leapt up into the air and flew away, leaving a terrible stench of burning and brimstone behind it. When the men examined the remains of the great black cats, they found that they were nothing but empty cat skins, with no flesh nor bones inside them. Murdo was helped down and taken to his home. He had escaped that night, not from the twelve great black cats and the huge red one, but from Auld Clootie, the Devil himself, and his demons out of hell.

Murdo had learned a valuable lesson that night, and he never again laughed at his fellow fishermen's superstitions. And he never went fishing on All Hallows E'en again for the rest of his days.

THE CASTLE OF THE SEAFARER

West Highlands

The ruins of an ancient castle stand by the edge of a tall, grey cliff overlooking the sea. They have stood empty for years beyond measure, and the wind and rain, the frost and the snow, have taken their toll on those once-strong walls. The roof fell long ago, so there is nothing left now but a shell. The wind moans and sighs where once there was laughter and song. For you see, the castle was once a place filled with light and joy, with warm fires and tables groaning under the weight of the food and drink piled upon them. Yes, this was a place where hospitality reigned supreme and everyone was welcome.

Below the cliff the sea surged and churned, yet to one side the land dipped and there was a beach of white sand and a strand of shingle that formed a little harbour. A road made of crushed stones ran down from the castle to this beach. There were once fishermen's cottages built along the skirts of the cliff above the high-water mark, like chicks nestled for protection under a hen. But they too are gone, as are the fisherfolk who once lived, loved and died there.

The name by which the castle was once known has long been forgotten, but its crumbling walls were used as a landmark by generations of fishermen who hauled their nets along that coast. They had a name for it; they called it *dùn na cuantaiche*, the Castle of the Seafarer. No one goes near it now, for there is a sadness there that never sleeps. The story that I will tell you has been passed down by these honest, hard-working folk, from one generation to the next.

The last laird to live in the castle was a sea captain with a fine ship of his own. But he was no merchant, carrying cargos and conducting trade. No, he had a spirit that craved adventure and danger. He was a privateer, a mercenary with letters from the crown that allowed him to attack enemy ships. Without these letters he would be regarded as a pirate and the rope would be his reward for capture.

The Captain, as he was known, also held true to the old tradition of Highland hospitality, and all were welcome at his castle. Regardless of whether he was in residence or not, his servants had their orders that if anyone called, they should be treated well with food, drink, and a warm bed to sleep in. He was famous for his hospitality.

One day, he returned from a voyage loaded up with gold and jewels from his latest conquest, and he started to prepare himself to greet any guests who might be there. His servant brought up more logs for the fire and warm water for the Captain to wash with. After he had washed and dressed in a fine suit of red velvet, the Captain asked his servant what guests were there for him to welcome.

'Och, the usual crowd,' said the servant, 'who have come to welcome you home. Oh, but there are some others, too. There's a couple from Edinburgh who say that they are your cousins. They have brought their daughter with them.'

The Captain left his room and walked down the stairs, ruffling his lace collar and cuffs as he went. He was a very handsome man and he liked to look good. He smiled as he walked down, because an old memory had stirred in his mind. These cousins of his would be the Frasers, who were distant cousins of his mother, so not close kin. He remembered going to visit them in Edinburgh with his mother when he was just a lad. The daughter, he recalled, was a wee thing, as round as a dumpling, tangled red hair and with a complexion the colour of whey. She was always eating sweets and had pawed at him once with her sticky fingers, the memory of which made him shudder.

On entering the grand hall, he cheerfully greeted his neighbours, who were keen to hear his latest adventures. Then his

Fraser cousins were brought forward, and he welcomed them warmly to his home. The mother smiled and said, 'You will, no doubt, remember our daughter Catriona?'

A young woman stepped forward, but she was no wee dumpling with a yellowish tinge to her skin. She was tall, slim, graceful, elegant, and had the bearing of a queen about her. Her complexion was as white as the snows in winter, her eyes deep blue, her lips as red as a rose and her teeth were like a row of pearls. Cascading over her shoulders and down her back was her beautiful red hair, which resembled copper and gold spun together to perfection. It contrasted with the green velvet dress that she wore, which enhanced its colour and radiance. The Captain stood rooted to the floor. Never before had he seen such a beautiful woman.

Catriona remembered the restless boy who had once visited them. He was brash, unruly and careless with everything he touched. But now, here before her stood a handsome young man with a finely chiselled chin and a muscular body, like a Greek statue. He had black, curly hair, dark eyes and a kind and tender look that melted her heart. The two young people stood there gazing at each other, forgetting that anyone else was in the room with them. No one noticed, but in those few short seconds love's dart had found its mark. They only had eyes for each other.

The Captain and Catriona danced at the ball that he had arranged in her honour. There was hardly a time when you didn't see the red and green velvet of their clothes entwined as they danced the night away. Her copper and gold hair shone in the candlelight, as they laughed joyfully together. He wooed her with songs and poems, and his words became more and more loving. She responded with pleasure. She felt her life had just begun, a new life with this beautiful man who adored her, and who she adored in equal measure.

Time passed, but the love that had made its home in their hearts remained, growing stronger with each passing hour. A gorgeous white silk wedding dress was ordered for the lovely bride-to-be. The castle had a wedding the like of which it had never known before. The couple where so happy that they had found each other, and it showed on their faces. Their joy was complete. They had given their hearts to each other. But that was a problem.

The Captain had no right to give his heart to Catriona, for it was not his to give. He already had a love, and one who would never give him up. For, you see, the Captain's first love was the sea. He was devoted to her, and no earthly love was strong enough to break that bond. It had started early, when he was just a baby. When his old nurse would carry him down to the sandy beach, he would laugh and clap his hands with joy at the sight of the white-capped waves as they broke on the shore. As a laddie, he was always down at the beach or playing among the fishing boats. He would spend hours staring at the sea from his window when he was meant to be doing his lessons. When he was half-grown, he persuaded his father to buy him a boat of his own and he would sail up and down the coast. Some nights, he would slip out of the castle to join the fishermen as they fished the seas. Yes, the sea had his heart first, which Catriona was soon to discover.

They had only been married for two months when he announced to Catriona that he was going to sea again. She protested.

'So soon?' she said. 'But we have not long been married, *mo gràidh* (my love).'

'Och, I'll come back to you,' he said with a laugh. 'I won't be away for long, *mo bhean gholach* (my beloved wife), just a month or two, that's all.'

Catriona raged at him, she begged him, she wept, but it was to no avail. He just shook his head and said, 'You knew that I was a sea captain before we wed. Did you not think that I would go back to sea?'

'Do you not love me, *mo gràidh*?'

'I love you, *mo bhean gholach.*' But as he spoke his eyes were fixed on the window, from where he could see the sea. He listened to the sound of the waves as much as he listened to Catriona's pleas.

'You love the sea more than you love me.'

He had no answer to give her, for what she said was true. In a couple of days, he kissed her farewell and left his castle. He walked down the stony road to the shore and took the boat out to where his fine ship lay at anchor in the shelter of the bay. The sea took the ship in its arms and carried it away from the weeping bride.

In a month or two, he returned with tales of adventure about the ships that he had raided, and the treasures won. He opened a small chest and poured the contents into Catriona's lap. Gold and jewels cascaded down, and he laughed to see such riches on the knee of the woman that he loved. But she remained unmoved by his words. She stood up, spilling the treasure onto the floor.

'I care nothing for these baubles,' she said. 'I would rather have my husband at home. I would sooner be a poor woman married to a ploughman and struggling to survive, but to have you here with me always.'

But she knew that it was only a matter of time before he left her again. Once the sea called, he would run to her. If his other love had been a mortal woman, then she could at least fight for his affections. But she could not fight the sea. Two years went by. Two years of her husband leaving her weeping in the castle. Two years of longing for his return. Then one day, he kissed her farewell for the last time. For he did not return.

Time passed. Catriona watched and wept, but her beloved husband did not come back. The ship was overdue, but no one dared to suggest to her that this time the sea had claimed him for good. Finally news came. A ship that had landed down the coast at Greenock had sent a message with a rider. He had no details, just something about a battle and a storm, he thought, but what he knew was that the Captain had been lost at sea.

The grief was almost too much for Catriona to bear. She locked herself away in her room and refused to see anyone. Any visitors, come to offer their sympathies, were given food and wine and then politely sent away.

When the mourners had stopped calling, Catriona rose from her bed of sorrow and left her room. She went here and there around the castle, but the servants shrank from her. She was dressed in a black velvet dress with her copper-gold hair hanging loose down her back, but it seemed as if she didn't belong to this world. She looked fey, like a fairy exiled from her kingdom. The servants felt great pity, but they also held a little bit of fear at the sight of her.

One day, she called the servants together and said, 'I no longer need your services, and I would like you to go and find work elsewhere. I will pay you well for the good service that you have done for me and for my husband.'

'But m'lady,' they protested, 'we don't want to leave you all alone here. It wouldn't be right to do such a thing. If money is lacking in your coffers, then don't worry about that. We will work for you all the same.'

But she said, 'I have rooms filled with riches and land and houses elsewhere. I was not a poor lass when I came here, and I am not troubled with money yet. I am going away from here. I will close up the castle and live somewhere else. I may never return here again.'

Sadly, the servants took the money she pressed on them and left the castle for good. Catriona did not leave the castle, but stayed in her room, gazing tearfully out to sea. Her grief never abated. Day and night she wept for the man she had loved – the man she still loved.

One day, as the sun was setting in the west in a blaze of red splendour, Catriona saw a sight that made her blood run cold. There, at its usual anchorage, lay a ship that she had seen before. In fact, she had seen it many times, coming and going, bringing her love back to her and then away again from her arms. It was the Captain's ship. She froze, her stare fixed to that accursed vessel. Soon she heard the sound of footsteps on the stone road outside and a knock at the door. She went down the great staircase and opened the door, her heart pounding. There on the doorstep were three sailors, each one carrying a small chest. Two were older men, burnt brown with the sun and the wind, every inch the sailor. But there was also a young lad who looked like he belonged on a croft, with fresh, ruddy cheeks and a mop of brown, curly hair.

'Begging your pardon, m'lady, but we come with news.'

Silently, she gestured for them to come in. They set down the three chests on the huge table in the hall, and the eldest one spoke again.

'We served for the Captain, your husband, and he told us that if anything happened to him then we were to bring you this and the ship.'

The sailors opened the chests, and they were filled with gold and gems of all sorts.

'Why have you brought me this?' she said, sharply. 'I have plenty of riches here. And what would I do with that accursed ship? It is of no use to me. I would have appreciated it more if you had brought my husband back, alive and well.'

'Oh, I wish with all my heart that I could do that, m'lady, for we all loved him too, and would have followed him to hell and back. Pardon my language, m'lady. But we are just following the Captain's orders. You see, we had attacked a treasure ship and it put up a stiff fight, but we overcame it in the end and this is what we got. But after we left it, the wind got up and there was a terrible storm. I've never seen waves as big as I saw that night, so help me! The Captain was at the wheel, when a huge wave swept over the stern of the ship and carried him away. We managed to grab him, but we couldn't hold him. The sea claimed him, and we had not the strength to fight the sea. No one has.'

A rage now rose in Catriona's breast. Why did these sailors return here, alive and well, and her husband lying dead at the bottom of the sea? Did they really try to save him? Or were they acting out of guilt, because it was their fault that he died? Yes! That was it. They killed him, just as sure as if they had stuck a dagger in his heart. They wouldn't get away with it. No! She would have her revenge on them. Oh yes, she would have her revenge!

'You must be hungry. Come, let me show you hospitality. My husband was famous for his hospitality.'

So saying, she led the three sailors towards the guard room of the castle. It was strong, to withstand attack, with one window high up and secured with strong bars, and a door of oak and iron. They sat at the table while she brought them food: bread, cheese and meat. Then she brought them wine to drink. But she had poured a sleeping draught into it first, one so strong that they would never know what happened to them. They thanked her and then ate the food and drank the wine.

First their speech became slurred and their movements clumsy. Soon, they were all fast asleep with their heads on the table. Catriona smiled and locked the door with the large iron key. They would never leave that room. They would pay for their treachery with their lives.

She left the castle carrying the key with her, and went to the edge of the cliff. She threw the key as far as she could so that it would be lost in the sea below. Even if the rest of the crew came to the castle, they would never get their friends out of that room, and the prisoners certainly could not get out.

Catriona went back to the castle and climbed the stairs to her room. She sat there for some time, brooding on what she had done.

Night came, and the moon rose. A shaft of moonlight entered the room and shone on the door that stood open before her. It was then that she noticed a movement in the doorway. She looked and saw the figure of a man standing there. It was no stranger, but her own beloved husband. At first, she thought that he was alive, come back to her, but then she saw the sea water dripping from his clothes, and the seaweed caught in his hair, and she knew he was dead. His eyes, too, had not the lustre of life in them, and when he spoke his voice was that of the grave, hollow and chilling.

'Oh, my poor, foolish dear,' he said. 'What have you done? Why did you treat my honest sailors so badly? What had they ever done to you? You should have thanked them and sent them away with a rich reward for their honesty. They came to you because I told them to, and now you must set them free.'

It was then that the insanity of her actions was revealed to her. Her mind cleared and she realised that she had wanted someone to blame and so had chosen them, although they had done her no harm.

'Oh, my God!' she cried. 'What have I done! I cannot open the door and set them free, because I threw the only key into the sea.'

'That is why I came here tonight,' he said. 'I have brought you back the key.'

So saying, he stretched out his arm and offered her the key. She took it. It was cold and wet, but she was overjoyed to see it again. Looking at the ghost of her husband, she pleaded, 'Stay with me!'

'That I cannot do,' he said. 'Listen.'

She listened, but all she could hear was the surge of the sea. Then she heard it. It seemed that the sea was calling to him.

'O come, O come, O come,' it sighed, and she knew that he would return to the sea. Her heart felt like it was breaking all over again, although it was still in pieces.

She looked at her husband with tears and said, 'Oh, do you not love me, *mo gràidh?*'

'I love you, *mo bhean gholach*.'

The tears flowed like streams from her eyes until she was blinded by them. When she wiped her eyes she found herself alone again. He was gone. Gone back to the sea.

Catriona walked back down the stairs, carrying the big iron key. She came to the door of the guard room and slid the key into the lock. She held her breath for a moment as she turned the key in the door, but the bolt of the lock drew back with a click. A wave of relief washed over her as she swung open the door. There at the table the three sailors were still fast asleep, unaware of the danger that they had been in. Quickly, she gave them a gentle shake to wake them up. With many yawns and stretches they awoke, full of apologies for having fallen asleep.

'Never you worry about that,' said Catriona, 'but the sun is rising and the tide is turning. You must be on your way again.'

'Where would you have us go, m'lady?' asked the elder sailor. 'With the dear captain gone, we have to take our orders from you. You own the ship now.'

Catriona looked at the man thoughtfully. It seemed to her that he was born on the sea. It was in his veins. She knew the signs well.

'Do you men love the sea?' she asked.

The elder man looked puzzled by her question, saying, 'Why, of course I do. I have known no other life but that of a sailor, nor would I ever want to. I wouldn't have been at sea for so long if I didn't love it.'

'And you?' she asked the other older man.

'Why, yes, I suppose I do. I have never given it a thought before. It never occurred to me. Yes, I do indeed love the sea.'

And then Catriona turned to the young lad with the ruddy cheeks and curly brown hair, saying, 'And what about you, young man. Do you love the sea?'

'No!' he said. 'I don't. I hate the life of a sailor.'

'So why do you go to sea?' she asked.

'Because my father before me and his father before him were sailors. I wanted to stay on land and become a farmer. I wanted to follow the plough and not the winds and tides. But my father signed me up, so that's why I'm here.' He looked thoughtful and added, 'I was just lucky, that's all, for he signed me up to your dear husband's ship. I could not have wished for a better master than he. Now that he's gone, begging your pardon m'lady, I dread returning to it. I just want to smell the soil, not the salty brine.'

Catriona smiled at him kindly and said, 'You are not a sailor, and the sea will not have you.'

'You're right there, m'lady,' said the elder man, 'he will never make a good sailor, if he were to be at sea for a hundred years.'

'Then let us spare him that fate,' said Catrina. 'My dear men, you have carried out my husband's wishes, now you shall carry out mine. To the two of you sailors I want to give one chest of treasure in payment. I also want you to have the ship. It is of no use to me. I will give you the ship's papers and I will write a letter granting full ownership to you both equally. No one can dispute it if it bears my signature and seal.'

The two men were astonished and refused to take such a huge reward for just following the Captain's orders. But Catriona's mind could not be changed. She added that this gift was by the orders of her husband. Eventually they accepted the gift with many fair words.

'Now you,' she said to the young lad, 'I want you to stay here for a short time as I have work for you to do.'

The young lad thanked her, again saying that the ship was not a place where he would feel happy now that his beloved master was gone.

'Make haste, ship masters, for the tide is on the turn and you must be away.'

The two sailors who loved the sea picked up the chest of treasure and headed down the stony road to the shore. She went with them for part of the way, along with the lad. She watched them row to the ship, weigh anchor and sail from the bay. She watched the ship until it was a speck on the horizon, and then it was gone. The two of them returned to the castle, where she asked more questions of the lad.

'Do you have a farm, or the chance of having one, some day?'

'Why, I have no money to buy a farm. My people are poor and owned no land. But my godfather has a farm, and not a small one. I have always dreamed that one day I might earn enough at sea to buy it from him. He has no sons, you see, and looks on me as family, so I would care for him in his old age.'

'Well, that can be easily remedied,' she said. 'Here, take the second chest of treasure and buy that farm. Work on the land and never set foot on a ship again. It is likely that your friends will fall victim to the sea, but you, at least, shall be spared.'

The lad also refused, but she repeated that it was her husband's orders, and that she had rooms full of riches, so one small chest would not be missed.

'You can go now,' she said, 'but you don't have to walk. In the stable there is a small black mare. You can ride her. Keep her, but take good care of her, never harness her to a carriage and never yoke her to a plough. She will serve you well for riding into town, or to the church on a Sunday.'

The lad thanked her many times before he went to the stable and saddled his horse. She watched him as he rode up the brae. When he reached the bend in the road, he turned and waved at her, then was gone.

'That is one that the sea will not have,' she said to herself, before returning to the castle.

Catriona picked up the third chest of treasure and climbed the stairs to her room. There was only one more thing for her to do. She put on her silken wedding dress and combed her copper hair. She opened the chest and gazed at the riches that it contained.

First she put golden, bejewelled rings on all her fingers. Next she fasten jewel-encrusted bracelets around her wrists. Then she bedecked herself with necklaces of gold, studded with diamonds, emeralds, sapphires and rubies. Last of all, she put a golden coronet on her head. She looked like a queen.

She stopped to look out the window at the sunlight sparkling on the sea. 'I have done all that I can here,' she said with a sigh. 'Now there is nothing left for me.'

With elegance and grace, she lay down on the silken coverings of her bed. The gold and gems sparkled in the morning light, but what shone brighter still were the tears that were in her eyes. She had once been so happy here. She had once loved so deeply. All was now just memories and nothingness. She closed her eyes, and at last grief stopped the broken pieces of her heart from beating. The sound of the sea against the shore was the last thing that she heard as she died.

The Captain and Catriona had no children, so the castle and all the estate passed to a distant cousin. They tried to live in the castle, but couldn't bear it. Many others tried too, but found it impossible to be happy there. They could not stand the ghostly cries of the beautiful Captain's wife, who glided through the castle from dusk to dawn, calling to her love to come back to her from the sea.

It was not only the castle owners who were troubled by the grieving ghost of Catriona, for the fisherfolk heard her too. The blood in their veins ran cold when they heard her cry. In time, one by one, they left. Some found a new place to stay in Barra, where they still worked as fishermen. It was a long way from the castle, so they could not hear her cries, and their children could sleep soundly in their beds. Eventually, the houses by the cliffs fell into ruin as well, crumbling away over time. Then, one night during the spring tide when the sea is at its highest, a storm blew from the west, bringing huge waves with it. All of the ruins of the houses were swept away into the sea so not a trace of them remains, only the walls of the old castle.

That is the story that the old fisherfolk told, many years ago. But if you pressed them further, they might tell you a bit more, although they didn't like to talk about it. They said that on a calm night with a soft wind from the sea, as they sailed by the cliffs where *an dun na cuantaiche* stands, they could hear voices on the wind – the broken-hearted wife called to her husband, who answered her from beneath the waves.

'Oh, do you not love me, *mo gràidh*?'

'I love you, *mo bhean gholach*.'

DEATH IN A NUT

West Highlands

For the folk who live on the coast, the sea can give as well as take. A keen eye is kept on the incoming tide, which may be the bearer of gifts. A plank of wood here, a length of rope there, part of the cargo of a ship that the sea had claimed; it could be anything, or nothing at all. Beachcombing is still something that people do today, but we don't rely on it like folk used to do in the past.

One beachcomber was a lad called Jack. Now, Jack lived with his mother in a small cottage by the shore. He didn't really remember his father, who had died when he was just a wee laddie, but his mother told him stories about his father, so Jack felt like he knew him well. Now it was just the two of them, making a living as best as they could.

Jack's mother kept ducks and hens, and they sold their eggs in the village. Jack's mother was well known for her fine green or white duck eggs, which had a wonderful flavour all of their own. The brown hen eggs were popular too, but they didn't fetch the price that the duck eggs did. Jack's mother also kept a few goats, which gave them milk that they turned into butter and cheese. Some they sold, some they kept for themselves. Jack cut hay in the meadow for them and tended them with love. He was a kindly soul, and very loving towards his mother and the creatures in his care. His mother also earned a few shillings mending clothes or knitting socks. They were poor in worldly goods, but rich in many other ways.

One winter's morning before the sun had risen, Jack got up and lit the fire and boiled the kettle to make a cup of tea. He knew that the tide was coming in and he wanted to be the first on the shoreline in case it brought something good. He would bring back anything that he found, in the belief that it might come in useful someday. What he mostly brought home was driftwood for the fire, which sparked wildly because of the salt that was in it.

When the kettle boiled, Jack made the tea, and he brought a cup to his mother. It was always his custom to fetch her a cup of tea when she was still in bed.

This morning she opened her eyes and when she saw the tea she shook her head, saying, 'I don't want a cup of tea, Jack.'

'Why not?' Jack asked. 'Are you ill or something?'

'Aye, Jack, I'm not feeling very well. In fact, I am very sick.'

'What's wrong with you? Are you in pain?'

'I don't know what's wrong with me, Jack, but I am feeling very ill and weak. I don't think that I have long left.'

'Here,' said Jack, 'try to take a sip of tea.'

He raised her head gently, and held the teacup to her mouth so she could take a sip.

She only managed two or three before she said, 'That's enough, laddie. I can't take any more.'

Now, Jack was worried because he had never seen his mother like this before. Something must be seriously wrong with her to keep her in her bed.

The old woman smiled. 'You know, Jack, we can't go on forever. It's not the way of things. I feel that he is coming to take me, very soon.'

'Who's coming to take you?'

'Och, you know fine who I mean, Jack. Now, listen, we have never had any secrets from each other, and we won't have any now. I am dying, Jack. I can feel it in my aching bones. The one who is coming for me is Death. But he will make things better, and take me to a place where there is no pain or sorrow.'

The hot tears streamed down Jack's cheeks. 'But you can't die, Mother! You can't leave me here alone. I have no friends or anyone to talk to. If you die, then I would be better off dying as well.'

'Hush now, Jack. You are a big lad and are capable of looking after yourself. One day you might meet a girl who will love you, like I have always done, and get married. But don't talk about death yet. You are young and fit and will live for many more years to come.' Jack's mother gave a great sigh and said, 'Leave me now, Jack. I am tired and would like to try to sleep a little more.'

Jack leant over and gently kissed his mother on her forehead. She smiled contentedly and was soon asleep. Jack left the cottage and headed down to the shore. His heart was breaking, but he knew that there was nothing he could do. He walked along the shore, looking for anything that had been brought in on the tide, but it was as empty as he felt inside.

It was then that Jack saw a stranger walking along the shore towards him. He was an odd-looking character, wearing a long, grey robe that was all tattered. His face was thin and pinched and his eyes were deep-set in his skull. His bare arms and legs were skeletal thin, and over his back he carried a scythe. The scythe looked shiny and new and razor sharp. It didn't take Jack long to figure out who this stranger was. It was Death.

'Hello, old man,' said Jack. 'Where are you off to so early on a winter's morning?'

'Hello Jack. Is it far to the next cottage?'

'No, it's not far,' said Jack, not the least surprised that the stranger knew his name. 'Why do you want to go there?'

'There's an old woman that I must take away with me.'

The fury rose in Jack's breast, and he shouted, 'I know who you are! You're Death, and you've come to take my mother away from me.'

Death looked sorrowfully at Jack. 'But Jack, it is her time. It is just the natural way of things. She is in pain, and I will take her to a place where she will never feel pain again. She will be at peace.'

Jack's anger just grew hotter. 'I won't let you take her!' he shouted. 'She is all I have, and I love her. You'll not have her this day.'

And so saying, Jack grabbed the scythe from Death, ran towards a big stone, and smashed the scythe against it. Now it was Death's turn to feel angry.

'My boy, you've done a foolish thing, but you have not won yet. This is not the end of the matter.'

'Well, it'll be the end for you!' shouted Jack, and he leapt on Death.

The two of them wrestled among the rocks and seaweed in a bitter struggle. Jack was a strong young man, but he was amazed at how strong Death was. They were well matched, as they fought on the strand. Jack saw a piece of wood that would make a good weapon. He grabbed it and began to beat Death with it. Then a strange thing happened, for Death showed no effects from the attack. No blood flowed, no bruises showed, but what did happen was that Death got smaller and smaller with every stroke. Jack kept beating him until Death shrank to the size of a toddler. Still Jack beat him, until he shrank to the size of the nail on Jack's little finger.

Triumphantly, Jack held Death between his finger and thumb and laughed. 'You'll not get my mother now, will you?'

If Death said anything in reply, he was too small to be heard. But Jack knew that if he let Death go, he would still get his mother. If he put him under a rock, he would crawl out and go about his business as usual. No, Jack had to find something to imprison him in.

As if by magic, Jack saw something strange among the seaweed that did not belong there. He picked it up and saw that it was a large hazelnut shell. In one side was a hole, which had been nibbled though by a red squirrel. They leave a neat, round hole in a hazelnut shell when they eat the kernel. This was just what Jack was looking for. He took the tiny Death and pushed him through the hole, head first. Then he found a stick and he broke it to form a stopper to seal the hole.

With Death safely inside the nutshell he said, with a laugh, 'I'd like to see you get out of that!'

Jack went to the water's edge and threw the nutshell, with Death imprisoned inside, as far out to sea as he could. The nutshell flew through the air and landed in the sea with a small plop, then it bobbed away on the ebbing tide. Happy with his morning's work, Jack set off for home, carrying the broken scythe with him.

As he approached the tiny cottage where he lived, Jack could see quite a lot of smoke coming from the chimney. His mother must be up, he thought. When he entered the house, he saw his mother baking a scone over the fire and smiling cheerfully.

'Are you feeling better now, Mother?'

'Aye, Jack, I never felt better in my life! It was strange – I was feeling so ill and weak and I thought my time had come, then the next thing that I knew, I felt wonderful. I just can't understand it.'

Jack smiled because he knew why she had recovered, but he said nothing about his encounter with Death. He sat down and ate his wee scone. Strangely, it did nothing to take away the hunger he was feeling.

'What else is there to eat, Mother?'

'Why don't you go and get a couple of hen eggs for us to fry for breakfast.'

So, Jack headed out to the hen house. The nest boxes were filled with lovely brown hen eggs. He took four and went back inside.

'I got four eggs, Mother. Two for you and two for me. That will fill us up nicely.'

His mother took a piece of pig fat and set it in the pan to melt. The piece of fat sat there, doing nothing. More sticks were added to the fire, but still the fat would not melt.

'I have never seen such a thing as that before,' said Jack's mother. 'That fat will just not melt.'

'Och, never mind the fat, Mother, just crack the eggs into the pan and give them a good stir around. I'm hungry.'

Jack's mother took an egg and tapped it against the edge of the pan to crack the shell, but nothing happened. She tried again, harder this time, but the egg didn't break. *Thunk!* went the egg on the edge of the pan, but still nothing. It was as if the eggshell was made of iron. Jack tried to break it too, but with no more success than his mother.

'Why don't you try boiling them, Mother?'

'Good idea, Jack.'

Jack's mother set them in a pot of water and boiled the eggs. They were stone cold when she took them out, and she couldn't get the top cut off them.

'Well, Jack, if we can't have an egg, you go and pull some vegetables and I'll make some soup.'

Jack went out to the garden, where he grew vegetables for their own use, and he pulled up a couple of carrots and some leeks and also some parsley. He brought them in to his mother, who washed them, but when she tried to chop them, the knife wouldn't cut through them. It just bounced off, like they were made of solid stone.

'They must be frozen,' said Jack's mother.

'But there hasn't been any frost,' Jack replied.

'Oh, well, we'll have to eat one of those young cockerels. We have far too many of them. Go and pull the neck of one of them.'

Jack went back to the hen house and looked at the line of young cockerels standing on the perch. He selected the largest, fattest one and he pulled its neck – nothing happened. He tried again, but still nothing. Eventually, he took the cockerel by the neck and swung it around and around his head several times, but still nothing happened. He went in and told his mother that he couldn't kill it.

'Och, you're getting soft-hearted, Jack. Why, you've killed hundreds of cockerels in the past.'

'It's not that I can't bring myself to do it, I just can't kill it.'

'Go and fetch me the axe and I'll show you how it's done.'

Jack took the axe to his mother, and she set the cockerel's neck on a chopping block. Whack! She chopped its head clean off. But as soon as she took the axe away the head jumped up off the floor and reattached itself to the neck. She struck again and again, but always the head jumped back onto the cockerel's neck and it was still alive.

Jack's mother looked troubled.

'It's as if this place is enchanted,' she said, 'but we'll not be beaten! Here, take this shilling and go to the butcher and buy some meat.'

Jack headed off down to the village, but when he reached the village square there were lots of people standing around chatting to each other. One was saying that his garden was being overrun with caterpillars, but no matter how much he sprayed them they wouldn't die. Even boiling water had no effect on them.

Outside the butcher shop there was a strangely long queue at the door. The butcher was standing there, red faced, and protesting to the people. 'It's not my fault,' he said, 'I have just spent the last hour trying to kill an ox. No matter how hard I hit it on the head, it just falls to its knees and then stands right up again. I tried cutting the throat of a sheep, but the knife can't cut it. I took a delivery of twenty ducks, but when I try to chop off their heads they just jump back on again.'

'Can I get some meat for my mother, please,' said Jack.

'There is no meat in the shop!' the angry butcher replied.

'I'm hungry! We tried to boil an egg, but it wouldn't cook. I tried to kill a cockerel ...'

'I tried to kill ten cockerels,' cried the butcher, getting even redder in the face, 'but they just won't die! The village up the road say the same thing is happening there, too. They can't even eat an apple because they can't get their teeth into it. I don't know what has gone wrong with the world. It's as if nothing will die!'

A terrible realisation ran through Jack's body when he heard this. And he knew why. He set off home to his mother and told her all that he'd heard. With his head bowed, he said, 'Mother, it's all my fault.'

'Och, don't be daft, laddie. What makes you say that?'

'Because this morning I met Death on his road to take you, and I broke his scythe and then I beat him until he shrank to a tiny wee thing and I shoved him in a nutshell, then I plugged it to stop him from getting out, and I threw him as far as I could out to sea. But I don't care if I starve to death, for I would rather do that than lose you.'

Jack's mother looked at her son in disbelief, then she smiled, a warm, loving smile. She said softly, 'Oh, Jack, Jack, Jack, my dear laddie. Do you not realise what you've done? You've destroyed the very thing that keeps the world alive.'

'What do you mean, Mother, "keeps the world alive"? If I hadn't trapped him then you'd be dead by now.'

'Yes, Jack, I probably would be dead. But people would be able to get food, and the world would keep on going, as it should. But now it can't, because of what you've done.'

'But what am I going to do?'

'There is only one thing that you can do. You are a beachcomber, Jack, just like your father before you. You must hunt the shore, looking for that nutshell, and when you find it, you must let Death go.'

'But he'll come for you, Mother.'

'Aye, he might do indeed, but I will be happy to go with him to wherever he takes me, because I will be at peace and you will carry on living, as it should be. People can only eat what is dead. You see, Jack, without Death there can be no life.'

With a heavy heart, Jack walked back to the shore and hunted for that nutshell, but he didn't find it that day, nor the next or the day after that. He was hungry now, so very, very hungry. Mile upon mile he walked along the coast, searching among the seaweed, desperate to find that nutshell and to release Death once again into the world. Jack wandered the coast for more than a week.

After a long, fruitless search one day, Jack was just about home again when he sat down on the rock where he had broken Death's scythe. He sat there, with his head in his hands, weeping.

'Why was I such a fool?' he said. 'I have ruined the world. People are suffering because of me. I wish I had never done it. I didn't know just how important Death is. People fear him, but he is a good person who helps sufferers to leave this world of pain.'

Then, looking down, he saw a hazelnut shell lying by his feet, with a wooden plug sticking out of it. With a cry of joy, he picked it up and quickly pulled out the plug.

Death stuck his head out, out, blinking in the light. 'So, are you happy now, Jack?'

'No, I'm not happy.'

'You thought that you'd beaten me, and that everything would be wonderful without me in the world. But you have a lot to learn, Jack. You see, without me there is no life.'

Jack set Death down on a flat stone, and he started to grow again. Soon he was his former size once more. He was just as he had been when Jack first saw him, with his long, tattered robe, shrunken face, deep-set eyes and skeletal thin arms and legs.

Death looked kindly at Jack. 'I must thank you for letting me out again. But Jack,' said Death, 'you broke my scythe.'

'I've mended it for you,' said Jack. 'My mother made me do it. Come along with me and we'll go and get it.'

They went to Jack's house, and sure enough, the scythe was leaning against the wall, just as good as it ever was.

Death picked it up, spat on his thumb, and ran it along the blade. 'I see you've sharpened it for me, Jack. You've done a good job of it.'

'Now I suppose you'll go and take my mother away from me?'

'Well, Jack, you have been good to me, so I will be good to you. You did what you did out of love for your mother, and I can't fault you for that. I will leave your mother for a while yet. But I must go now, for I have a lot of work to catch up with. I'll go to the village first.'

With that, Death turned around and walked quietly away, while Jack went back indoors to tell his mother the good news.

Jack and his mother lived contentedly together for many more years after that. But one day, when Jack's mother was about one hundred years old, Death came back again and took her away as she slept. Jack didn't see him this time, but he resigned himself to the fact that she had lived beyond her allotted span of time. He also knew the most important thing of all: there is no life without Death.

THE PRINCESS OF LAND-UNDER-WAVES

West Coast

When the Scots came from Ulster to settle in the islands and lands to the west of the country that now bears their name, Scotland, they brought with them their stories. The land that they occupied was called Dalriada, and the Gaelic spoken there originated in Ireland. Among the ancient tales that they brought with them were the stories of the giants, the Fianna, led by Finn McCool (Fionn mac Cumhaill in the Irish tongue). While they were regarded as the guardians of Erin, they soon became firmly rooted in Alba's folklore and tales. Many sites are pointed out that were the homes of the Fianna, or connected in some way with the great warrior poets of ancient legends.

Under the sea lies a magical kingdom. It can be seen on a calm day when no breeze ripples the surface of the water and the sun shines brightly. Land-under-Waves is visible on such days, with its green valleys, bejewelled with brightly coloured flowers that never fade or die. This land has green forests and sparkling streams with silver sand, golden rocks and gems of all colours that glint in the light as the currents of the streams turn them over.

On one such day in May, the Fianna lay by the Red Cataract, where the salmon leaps, and they stared at Land-under-Waves, which was particularly bright that day. They gazed at the beauty of it in wonder, each wrapped in their own thoughts. Suddenly, they became aware that there was a small boat heading towards the shore, but they couldn't tell if it was on the surface of the sea or under it. The boat was being rowed with two oars and there was a solitary person on board. The Fianna had wonderful eyesight, like the hawk, but Finn's was the keenest of them all.

'It is a young lady who rows the boat, whose beauty is beyond all others that I have ever seen. The boat ploughs a furrow through the seas, which seems to stir the trees of Land-under-Waves with every stroke of the oar.'

The lady landed her boat on the shore, where the Fianna were waiting for her. She stepped lightly from the boat and walked towards Finn, who greeted her.

'My lady, from where have you come and to what tribe do you owe kinship?'

'I have come from Land-under-Waves, where my father is the king. I am in search of Finn McCool and the Fianna.'

'You are welcome, Princess of Land-under-Waves, and your quest is at an end.'

'Are you then Finn McCool?'

'Truly I am, indeed, and these are my warriors, the Fianna. But why do you seek me?'

'I am in mortal danger, and my enemy is hard on my heels. He is a mighty warrior, but I have said that Finn McCool will be my saviour and will vanquish my foe, for his deeds are renowned throughout many kingdoms.'

'You shall be protected by me and my warriors, fair maiden, but tell me, who is it that follows you?'

'He is a mighty warrior who has pursued me over the ocean. His name is Dark Prince-of-Storm, and he is the son of the White King of Red Shields. He means to seize my father's kingdom and to have me as his bride. I have defied him and swore that Finn McCool would fight for my honour.'

Then Oscar, the grandson of Finn, stepped forward and said, 'If Finn were not here, I would take up arms against the Dark Prince and deny him his prize.'

With those words the sky grew dark, and the Land-under-Waves was no longer visible. Away towards the west, on the horizon, they saw the huge figure of a man on a mighty steed.

The horse was blue-grey, like the sea, with a mane and tail like white sea foam. The rider spurred him on and the horse ran over the tops of the waves, sending up spray as it galloped towards the shore. On the warrior's head was a shining helmet and in his left hand he held a ridged shield, while in the right he held a huge sword. When the steed reached the shore the mighty warrior leapt from its back, onto the shore.

'Is this the man who troubles you?' asked Finn.

'It is indeed him, and no other,' replied the princess.

Goll, the old warrior, and Oscar, the youthful hero, sprang forward and put themselves between the Dark Prince and the princess. But he was reluctant to fight them; he headed for Finn, who was unarmed at the time. Goll threw a spear, which cleaved the warrior's shield in two. Oscar threw another spear, which killed the warrior's steed. It was considered a great deed, and Oscar's father, Ossian the bard of the Fianna, would write a song in honour of his son.

The Dark Prince roared in anger and demanded that fifty warriors should fight him all at one time. A great battle was held there on the shore, with warriors raining blows on the Dark Prince, who parried them with his huge sword. Then Goll stepped forward and the two of them engaged in fierce single combat. But Goll proved the mightier of the two, and he slew the Dark Prince, whose body lay upon the shore. Once the ocean giant had been killed, the sky cleared, the sun shone, and Land-under-Waves was visible once more.

The Princess of Land-under-Waves thanked Finn and the Fianna for saving her, then bade them farewell. Finn stepped into her boat and took her to the gateway of her kingdom, which was a sea cave on the Far Blue Isle.

Before she left him, the princess said, 'Promise me one thing, Finn McCool, that if I ever need you again then you will come to my aid and come fast.'

'You have my word, my lady.'

Then Finn returned to the Fianna, who celebrated the victory with a feast.

A year and a day later, on another calm morning, Finn and the Fianna were sitting under the Red Cataract, gazing at the beauty of Land-under-Waves, when a boat was sighted heading in their direction.

'Is that the Princess of Land-under-Waves?' asked Oscar.

'No,' said Finn, 'this is a man who is coming.'

When the boat reached the shore, Finn greeted the man.

'Who are you, stranger, and what brings you into my lands?'

'I am the messenger of the Princess of Land-under-Waves. She is gravely ill and is likely to die. She wishes to remind you of your promise to come to her aid when she is in need of it.'

The Fianna were sorrowful on hearing this news, as they cared for the princess like a daughter.

Finn replied, 'I have not forgotten my promise. What would you have me do?'

'Let Jeermit the Healer come with me to Land-under-Waves and work his skills at healing. He may yet save her life.'

It was agreed, and Jeermit went with the messenger in his boat. He was the son of Angus-the-Ever-Young, and the fairest of all the Fianna. His father had bestowed the gift of healing on him; he knew herb lore and how to use healing waters, and his touch could prevent someone from dying until he had found a cure.

They rowed to the Far Blue Isle, where they found the sea cave that was the entrance to Land-under-Waves. Darkness wrapped itself around them as the boat took them further and further towards the undersea world. It was dark for a long time before the light returned and the boat grounded on a distant shore. Before them was a broad, level plain, and the messenger led Jeermit across it. For miles and miles they journeyed, yet Jeermit never felt tired by the long walk. He saw a clump of red moss, and he picked some and placed it in his bag. He well knew its healing properties. He passed a second patch of red moss and gathered some of that too, likewise with a third patch.

Eventually they saw a castle made of gold.

'Whose castle is that?' asked Jeermit.

'That is the castle of the King of Land-under-Waves, and the princess lies inside, like to die.'

On entering the castle, Jeermit saw many courtiers, all with sad faces. The queen came and took him by the hand and led him to the bedchamber where the dying princess lay. She was as beautiful as he remembered, but so white and cold. He laid his hands on her and the healing power of his touch flowed through her body. She opened her eyes and smiled a sweet smile.

'I feel stronger already, but the sickness lies on me still and I fear that I will die.'

'Nay, my lady, you will not die. I have with me three portions of red moss, which you must take in a drink. They are the three life drops of your heart, and they will heal you.'

'Alas, I cannot drink them, for I can only drink from the cup of the King of the Plain-of-Wonder. A wise woman told me that a drink of healing water from this cup, mixed with the healing moss, will save me. The moss from the Wide-Bare-Plain you have found, but the magic cup you will never have.'

Jeermit knew of many healing things, but he had not heard of this cup before. 'Where can this cup be found?'

'It belongs to the King of the Plain-of-Wonder, whose kingdom lies next to my father's. But the two kingdoms are divided by a river that no one can cross.'

'I will find a way, my lady, and I will heal you.'

So saying, Jeermit placed healing spells on the princess, so that she would remain alive until he should return with the magic cup. The king and queen and all the people of the Land-under-Waves now smiled; he had given them hope. They bade him farewell, and he left the golden castle and walked alone to the river that divided the two kingdoms.

The river was wide and fast flowing, with no bridges over it. Jeermit walked along its banks, but he couldn't find any way to cross it. Frustrated, he cried out aloud, 'I cannot cross over! The princess spoke truly.'

As he spoke, a small man rose out of the river. His skin was wrinkled and weathered with the sun, like a piece of brown leather. His clothes were all brown, too. Then the little man spoke. 'Jeermit, you are in dire straits.'

'Indeed I am, you speak wisely.'

'What would you give to someone who could help you in your troubles?'

'I would give anything that they asked for.'

'All I ask for is your goodwill.'

'That you shall have, and freely given.'

'Then I shall carry you across the river.'

Jeermit looked at the little man in wonder, and shook his head. 'I fear that you could not bear the weight of me.'

'Oh, indeed I can. Climb up on my back.'

Jeermit did as he was told. To his amazement, the little man stood up and stepped onto the river, walking over the surface like it was made of stone. As they crossed they passed an island, over which hung a dark mist.

'What island is that?' asked Jeermit.

'That is the Cold-Isle-of-the-Dead. There is a well on the island whose water has great healing power.'

Soon they reached the far shore, and the little man set Jeermit down.

'You are going to fetch the Cup of Healing from the King of Plain-of-Wonder?'

'Yes, I am. To cure the princess.'

'I wish you luck. But do you know where you are?'

'I am in the kingdom of the Plain-of-Wonder, am I not?'

'Yes, true, you are. But it is also called Land-under-Mountains and lies next to Land-under-Waves.'

Jeermit was about to ask the little man a question, but he had disappeared under the waters of the river and was gone. He walked on, and he saw that although it was as bright as day, there was no sun in the sky. Yet it never grew dark in Land-under-Mountains. After a while, he saw a silver castle with a roof of crystal. The doors were shut and guarded by warriors.

He shouted, 'Open and let me in!'

One of the warriors went to meet him with his sword drawn, but Jeermit threw a spear at him and killed him. The doors opened.

King Ian came out, saying, 'Who are you, and where do you come from?'

'I am Jeermit, son of Angus-the-Ever-Young.'

'You are welcome, but why did you not send a message? It is a shame to lose so great a warrior.'

'Give him a drink from the Cup of Healing. There is no healing power in it unless it is in the hands of Angus or Jeermit.'

The golden cup was brought, and Jeermit held it to the dead warrior's mouth and poured in a few drops of the water. The warrior opened his eyes and sat up. He drank the rest of the healing water from the cup and stood up, alive once more, and his wound was healed.

Jeermit then turned to the king. 'I have journeyed here to find this cup, and I will take it with me now.'

'So be it!' said the king. 'I give it freely to you. But it now lacks the healing water, as my warrior has drunk it all.'

Jeermit's heart sank when he heard this, but he resolved to take the cup anyway.

Then the king said, 'I will give you a boat to cross the river and to pass the Cold-Isle-of-the-Dead.'

'I need no boat,' said Jeermit, 'but I thank you for the offer.'

There was something that Jeermit didn't trust about the king, although he had not been given any reason to doubt him.

'May you return soon,' said the king with a smile. He didn't believe that Jeermit could cross the river and would be forced to return.

He took his leave of the king and walked back to the raging river. There he sat with his head in his hands. He had obtained the cup, but without the healing water it was useless. Now he had no way of crossing the river.

'Alas!' he cried. 'I have failed in my quest. I have the cup, but not the healing water to cure the princess. I have no way of crossing this river and so will have to return to the King of Plain-of-Wonder in shame.'

Just then, the same small man rose from the water. 'You are again in dire straits, Jeermit,' he said.

'That I am, indeed,' said Jeermit. 'I have got the cup but lack the water to heal. I cannot cross the river and must return to the king as a shamed man.'

'Fear not, I will carry you over once more.'

So the small man took Jeermit up on his back and walked over the water. But this time his steps took them in another direction.

'Where are you taking me?'

'To the Cold-Isle-of-the-Dead. You wish to heal the princess, do you not?'

'Yes, I do, with all my heart.'

'Then you will need to fill the cup at the Well of Healing. Only then can you save the princess. But Jeermit, I warn you, you must not set one foot on the soil of that island, or it will mean your death. No mortal can survive its touch.'

He agreed, and the small man carried him to the island and to the Well of Healing, where he knelt by its side. Jeermit bent down and scooped up a cupful of water from the well and they went on their way.

Once they had crossed the river, the small man set Jeermit down, saying, 'Now your heart rejoices!'

'Indeed it does, thanks to you, my friend. But why have you helped me so much, and for no reward?'

'Because your heart is warm, and you desire to help others. Any man who possesses such gifts will always find a friend, whether in the Land of the Living, the Land of the Dead, the Land-under-Waves or the Land-under-Mountains. But before we part, I will give you one last piece of advice. When you give the Water of Healing to the princess, she will not be cured until you add three pieces of red moss to it.'

'I have already found those, my friend.'

'That is good. But I will offer you this advice as well. When the princess is cured, the King of Land-under-Waves will offer you gifts. Take nothing from him but ask for a boat to take you home. He will want you to marry the princess, but if you ever wish to return to your home and to your family and friends, then just ask for the boat.'

Jeermit thanked the small man, and they parted as friends. He walked on until he reached the castle of gold, where he was led to the princess's bedchamber. She smiled a sweet smile when he came in carrying the Cup of Healing.

'I never expected you to return, but my heart is glad that you have. No man has ever held that cup before in this realm.'

Jeermit dropped in the three portions of red moss, the three life drops of her heart. He mixed it, held it between his healing hands and spoke spells over it, then he gave it to the princess to drink. She took three sips, each one containing a piece of the moss, and she was cured.

'I am healed!' she said. 'Now, let us feast and I will sit at board with you.'

And so it was. Where there had been sorrow before there was now joy and laughter.

The king laughed most heartily of all. 'I must reward you for saving my daughter. Have as much silver and gold as you like! You may marry my daughter and be the heir to my kingdom.'

'But if I do that then I can never return to my home, to my family and friends.'

'That is so. You can only return on very short visits, if at all.'

'Then I would ask a gift from you, as my reward, although it is only a small thing.'

'Ask and it shall be yours. You have my promise.'

'I would like a boat to take me back home, to Finn and the Fianna. I miss my homeland dearly, and my comrades in arms.'

'I grant it freely.'

Jeermit bade farewell to the king and queen and to the princess, who said, 'I shall never forget you, Jeermit, son of Angus-the-Ever-Young. You found me suffering and you brought me relief. You found me dying and you gave me life. When you return to your own land, think of me, for I will be thinking of you with every hour of every day, and I will be joyful and thankful for you.'

Jeermit left the castle and walked over the Wide-Bare-Plain, back to the harbour where the boat was moored and the boatman was waiting. He rowed Jeermit back to the entrance of the sea cave on the Far Blue Isle, and then over the sea to his own land. Finn saw him coming and gathered the Fianna to welcome him home.

When the boat reached the shore, Finn said, 'Welcome home, Jeermit. We feared that you would never return.'

'How long have I been away?'

'Seven long years.'

Jeermit thought that he had only been away for a short time. 'There was no night and day in the land that I was in and no way of marking the passing of time. But I am glad to be back home among my own folk, where I belong.'

They went to Finn's hall where they feasted to celebrate Jeermit's return. He had brought with him the Cup of Healing, which he set up in the hall as a reminder of how he had saved the life of the princess of the Land-under-Waves.

AND FINALLY ...

THE STORYTELLER WITHOUT A STORY

Scottish Traveller Tale

It seems these days that some storytellers like to talk about themselves. It's the age that we live in, the age of 'self'. But if you'll indulge me for just a moment, I'd like to tell you a wee story about something that happened to me when I was young. Now, you might not believe it, but I swear it is as true as the sun rises in the west and the deep love that the government has for us poor folk.

I was born on a wee farm and it had been decided that I would work there with my eldest brother. I'm not sure when that was decided – I must have missed that meeting. It was probably my parents' way of keeping me out of the dock, as I had given up school at fourteen. I didn't particularly like being called names and beaten. And that was only the teachers!

Anyway, the farming life did not suit me and I decided that I had to go out into the world and find my destiny. Whatever that might be. I left Orkney and travelled along the coast, working here and there at whatever would put a pound in my pocket. I eventually came to a big farm that was hiring men to work in the hay. Now, I was not a big fan of farm work, but I was hungry and out of tobacco. I used to smoke roll-ups in those days, and I was fond of a pint and a dram. So, I took the job and I worked hard bringing in the bales of hay. It's all automated nowadays, but back then hay came in small, heavy, rectangular bales that had to be built in a barn or in a haystack. I could do that, and I did.

The farmer was a nice bloke and he asked me if I'd like to stay on the farm and work in the harvest. I agreed. That was even harder work, as it was all sheaves of oats that had to be carted to the stackyard and built into beehive-shaped stacks. It was cold work, often wet and back-breaking. But eventually it was all in, safe and secure, and this was a cause for celebration.

I lived in a small bothy with the other labourers. It was down at the coast, near to where the farmer's boat was secured. A proper cèilidh was organised, and it was great fun. There was beer aplenty and whisky, music, stories, songs and lots of laughter. Everyone did something to entertain the rest of us, but I just sat at the side and enjoyed myself.

As the evening wore on, the farmer leaned forward and said to me, 'Well, Tom, how about you do something now?'

'Ach, no. Sorry, but I am no good at any of that stuff. I can't play an instrument, and don't ask me to sing! There's a court order against me singing. No, I'll just sit here and listen.'

The farmer frowned. 'Tom, you know the old saying, don't you?'

Tell a story,
Sing a sang,
Show your bum
Or oot ya gang!

'Well,' I said, 'I don't know any stories, and I'm sure as hell not showing my bum!'

'Well,' said the farmer, 'we are all relieved to hear that! But come on, you must know at least one story?'

'No, I'm sorry, but I have no stories. Not one!'

'Well then, you will have to do a forfeit.'

'Oh aye,' I said, suspiciously, 'what sort of a forfeit?'

'You know my old boat, lying down there on the shore?'

'Aye, I know her fine.'

'Well, in the bow of the boat there is the bailer. You know, the wooden scoop that I use to bail the water out of the boat? I want you to fetch it back here to me. I need it for measuring out cattle feed tomorrow.'

'That's it?'

'Aye, that's it.'

Well, I was mightily relieved. It seemed as if I was getting off lightly. I picked up an old storm lantern, lit it, and headed out the door and down to the shore where the boat was sitting. I set the lantern down on the shore and looked into the boat. Sure enough, there was the bailer lying in the bow, just as the farmer had said. I stepped into the boat and walked towards the bailer. I had just leant forward to pick it up when, whack! I slipped on the bottom of the boat, smacked my head and I was out like a light.

When I regained consciousness, I realised that the boat was moving underneath me. It was as black as pitch and I couldn't see anything. I used an oar to measure the depth of water beneath the boat, but it wasn't long enough to touch the bottom. There was no sign of the shore or of any lights. I didn't know in which direction to go, but I decided that I would trust my luck and row in some direction. So, I put the oars in the rollocks and began to row the boat, but I didn't make much of it. I seemed to have lost my strength.

I stopped and thought to myself, 'I need a smoke,' so I put my hand to the chest pocket of my old denim work jacket.

My hand felt something there. A lump. A large, soft, warm lump. I was confused, and I moved my hand to the other side … and there was another one. I looked down, but instead of my old denim work jacket, I was wearing a white blouse. As I looked further down, I saw that instead of my jeans, I was wearing a skirt and there were slender legs coming out of it. I scratched my head, only to find that I now had long, flowing, silky hair. Slowly, it started to dawn on me. I was a woman!

I tried to row the boat, using one oar at a time, but I didn't make much progress. Exhausted, I sat in the bow of the boat and burst into tears. Eventually, I fell asleep. How long I slept, I don't know, but when I woke I found that the boat had drifted to another shore. Where that shore was, I had no idea. I became aware that there was a man on the shore, looking at me.

He walked over to the boat and said, 'Who are you? What happened to you?'

'I don't know. I must have come from a shipwreck. Yes, that's it, I was shipwrecked.'

'That doesn't look much like a lifeboat.'

'It wasn't much of a ship,' I said. I was always good with the one-liners.

'What's your name?'

Good question, I thought. 'Eh, er, mmm, Thomasina…' I said, hopefully.

'Well, Thomasina, you had better come up with me to the house and have something warm to eat. Your family must be frantic with worry. You can stay with me until they find you.'

Offering me his arm (for he was ever the gentleman), the stranger led me to his house. A modest enough little place down by the shore, but nice, all the same. On entering the lobby I saw myself in the mirror for the first time. Well, I don't like to boast, but I was HOT! I ate a hearty breakfast and then was shown a nice, soft bed, where I slept for a while. On waking up, the man was more than kind. He made me a cup of tea and brought out cake and biscuits, which were lovely. He chatted away for hours. He told me that his name was Andrew and that he had lived alone since the death of his parents. There were very few people in the neighbourhood, but he was happy enough working on the farm and he had a boat by the shore as well, which he went fishing with. He made a nice meal that evening and we talked by the fire until it was time for bed.

Time passed, and of course my family didn't come to claim me. They would have got the shock of their lives if they had found me. Anyway, Andrew was a total gentleman and we enjoyed each other's company. But he was only human, so he couldn't help falling in love with me, and who could blame him! One day he went down on one knee and asked me to do him the honour of being his wife.

I giggled and said, 'Aye, all right then.'

Well, what else could I do? The wedding came and I wore a beautiful, slim, silky white dress. It was the early 1980s, but I didn't want one of those huge meringue-like dresses that were all the rage. I was classy. We had a lovely wedding with all his family and friends and it was said by all that they had never seen a bride put away more whisky than me.

Time passed and I started to feel sick in the mornings. I also had a craving for fire lighters. Yes, I was pregnant, and had a lovely wee boy that we named Andrew, after his dad. More time passed and I had another wee boy that we called John, after my dad. We lived together in happiness and it seemed as if this life would go on forever. But it didn't.

One day, in midsummer, I was walking along the coast with Andrew arm-in-arm, when I saw something familiar on the shore. There was that boat that had brought me here, from one shore to another. Just then, there was a roll of thunder and a flash of lightning and the heavens opened. The rain fell in torrents and we ran for shelter underneath a tree. Andrew told me to wait there for him and he would run home for my coat, as I was just dressed in a light summer dress. As I said, ever the gentleman.

As I stood there I couldn't help but stare at the boat, and a thought crept into my head, like a thief in the night. 'I wonder if that bailer is still there?'

I ignored the rain and headed down to the boat. I looked inside and, sure enough, there was the bailer still lying in the bow. I stepped into the boat and walked towards the bailer, thinking, 'Ya wee devil! The trouble you have caused me!'

As I bent down to pick it up my foot slipped and whack! I banged my head and was out cold.

When I woke up, it was dark. I sat up and looked around. In the distance I saw a light and decided to row towards it. I noticed that I could now row as strongly as I ever could. I also noticed something else. The smell. It was not a pleasant one, but strangely familiar: sheep dip, stale sweat, cigarette smoke and old whisky. I realised that the smell was coming from me.

I looked down, and there was my old denim work jacket and jeans, and my heavy work boots. It then occurred to me that I was a man again. Once more, my response was to burst into tears. Well, who could blame me? I was happily married and had two wee laddies who I loved very much. If I was now back to who I had been before, then I'd never see them again.

I sat there for a while, deep in thought, before deciding to row towards the light once more. As I got nearer I started to recognise the shore and saw that the lamp was the storm lantern I had left there a good ten years before. It had certainly burned for a very long time! There was the farm bothy, just above the shore, with light coming from it and the sound of a party. I picked up the bailer and the storm lantern and walked up the slope to the house. I opened the door and saw, to my amazement, that all the same people were there. I went over to the farmer and handed him the bailer, then sat down.

'You look a bit white, Tom,' said the farmer. 'What's ailing you?'
'Oh, nothing,' I lied.

'I think there's something troubling you. What is it?'

I choked back the tears and told him the whole story. He sat there, impassively, listening to me.

'But that must have taken a long time, Tom.'

'Aye,' I said, 'Young Andrew is nine now and wee Johnny is six.'

'But you weren't away for that long. The clock said that it was twenty to twelve when you left. Look at it now.'

I looked at the clock and saw that it said twelve o'clock, midnight. But how could that be? I had been away for ten years. I had got married and had children. How was any of this possible?

The farmer looked at me with a strange smile on his face. I always thought that he knew more than he was letting on.

He leant forward, slowly, and said in a low voice, 'Well, Tom! If ever anyone asks you to tell a story, you'll have one to tell them now. Won't you?'

SOURCES

EAST AND NORTH COASTS

The Three Questions
Sheila Kinninmonth, *Fife Folk Tales*, 2017.
Based on a version I heard told many years ago, but I can't now remember who it was who told it. I am indebted to them nevertheless.

The Bell Rock
Erin Farley, *Angus Folk Tales*, 2021.

The Blackthorn Stick
Sorche Nic Leodhas, *Twelve Great Black Cats*, 1972.

John Reid and the Mermaid
Hugh Miller, *Scenes and Legends of the North of Scotland*, 1831.
Bob Pegg, *Highland Folk Tales*, 2012.

Why the Sea is Salt
Ernest Marwick, *An Anthology of Orkney Verse*, 1949. Based on a poem by Bragi the Skald, *c*.AD 850.
Tom Muir, *The Mermaid Bride and Other Orkney Folk Tales*, 1998.

The Mermaid's Cave
Ernest Marwick, *The Folklore of Orkney and Shetland*, 1975.

The Seal Hunter
Scottish Fairy Tales, Braken Books, 1993.

The Devil in Smoo Cave
Alan Temperley, *Tales of the North Coast*, 1977.
Judy Hamilton, *Scottish Myths and Legends*, 2003.
Bob Pegg, *Highland Folk Tales*, 2012.

NORTHERN ISLES

Orkney & Shetland

The Denschman's Hadd
Chambers's Journal of Popular Literature, Science and Arts, 23
October 1886.
Lawrence Tulloch, *The Foy*, 2006.

The Selkie Boy of Breckon
Lawrence Tulloch, *The Foy*, 2006.
I have based this on hearing Lawrence tell the story many times.

The Stolen Boots
Lawrence Tulloch, *The Foy*, 2006.
I have based this on hearing Lawrence tell the story many times.

The Trows' Boat Journey
Lawrence Tulloch, *Shetland Folk Tales*, 2014.
I have heard Lawrence tell that story before. I think he heard it

from George P.S. Peterson of Papa Stour. I liked the Shetland dialect word *pjag* (pronounced pee-yag) used to describe the stroke of the oar, but usually it means hard labour, often relating to digging.

The Selkie's Bargain
Sir George Douglas, *Scottish Fairy and Folk Tales*, 1893.
Lawrence Tulloch, *Shetland Folk Tales*, 2014.

Assipattle and the Mester Stoorworm
Sir George Douglas, *Scottish Fairy and Folk Tales*, 1893.
Walter Traill Dennison, *Orkney Folklore & Sea Legends*, 1995.

How the Mermaid Got Her Tail
Walter Traill Dennison, *The Scottish Antiquary or Northern Notes and Queries*, Vol. VI, 1893.
Walter Traill Dennison, *Orkney Folklore & Sea Legends*, 1995.

The Selkie Wife of Westness
Walter Traill Dennison, *Scottish Antiquaries*, 1893.
Walter Traill Dennison, *Orkney Folklore & Sea Legends*, 1995.

The Nuckelavee
Walter Traill Dennison, *The Scottish Antiquary or Northern Notes and Queries*, Vol. V, 1892.
Walter Traill Dennison, *Orkney Folklore & Sea Legends*, 1995.

The Selkie that Didn't Forget
Walter Traill Dennison, *The Orcadian Sketch Book*, 1880.

WESTERN ISLES

The Blue Men of the Minch
Donald Alexander Mackenzie, *Wonder Tales from Scottish Myth and Legend*, 1917.
Ian Stephen, *Western Isles Folk Tales*, 2014.

The Sea Cow
John MacPherson, *Tales from Barra told by Coddie*, 1992.

The Selkie Wife of Glendale
George W. MacPherson, *Highland Myths & Legends*, 2001.

The MacLeods of Raasay and the Witches of Skye
Gregor Ian Smith & Alasdair Alpin MacGregor, *Strange Stories and Folk Tales of the Highlands and Islands*, 1995.

The Cruel Skipper
A.J. Bruford & D.A. MacDonald, *Scottish Traditional Tales*, 1994.
The story was recorded from Peter Morrison, Grimsay.

The Spanish Princess and the Fairy Cats
Peter MacNab, *Tall Tales from an Island*, 1984.

The Barraman and the Witches
John MacPherson, *Tales from Barra told by Coddie*, 1992.

Tir-nan-Og
Gregor Ian Smith & Alasdair Alpin MacGregor, *Strange Stories and Folk Tales of the Highlands and Islands*, 1995.

Corryvreckan
Dr Patrick H. Gillies, *Netherlorn and its Neighbourhood*, 1909.
https://whirlpool-scotland.co.uk/legend
There are differing versions of this tale, growing with each telling. I have tried to stick as faithfully as possible to what seems to be the oldest version of this story, which I have heard from many sources over the years.

WEST COAST

The Devil and the Laird of Ardrossan
'The De'il of Ardrossan', Folklore Scotland, folklorescotland.com/the-deil-of-ardrossan.

The Mermaid's Curse
Sir George Douglas, *Scottish Fairy and Folk Tales*, 1893.
Judy Hamilton, *Scottish Myths and Legends*, 2003.
Taylor Petrie, https://folklorescotland.com/the-vengeful-mermaid

The Selkie's Revenge
Duncan Williamson, *Tales of the Seal People*, 1992.

The Demon Cats
Sorche Nic Leodhas, *Twelve Great Black Cats*, 1972.

The Castle of the Ocean
Sorche Nic Leodhas, *Twelve Great Black Cats*, 1972.

Death in a Nut
Duncan & Linda Williamson, *The Thorn in the King's Foot*, 1987.

The Princess of Land-under-Waves
Donald Alexander Mackenzie, *Wonder Tales from Scottish Myth and Legends*, 1917.

AND FINALLY ...

The Storyteller Without a Story
Sheila Douglas, *Last of the Tinsmiths, The Life of Willie MacPhee*, 2006.
I never had the pleasure of meeting Willie MacPhee, but it is said that he always told this story in the first person and when I tell this story I do the same, with semi-autobiographical details to fool the listener, at first.

BIBLIOGRAPHY

Bruford, A.J. & MacDonald, D.A., *Scottish Traditional Tales*, 1994.

Chambers's Journal of Popular Literature, Science and Arts, 23 October 1886.

Dennison, Walter Traill, *The Orcadian Sketch Book*, 1880.

Dennison, Walter Traill, *Orkney Folklore & Sea Legends*, 1995.

Douglas, Sir George, *Scottish Fairy and Folk Tales*, 1893.

Douglas, Sheila, *Last of the Tinsmiths, The Life of Willie MacPhee*, 2006.

Farley, Erin, *Angus Folk Tales*, 2021.

Gillies, Dr Patrick H., *Netherlorn and its Neighbourhood*, 1909.

Hamilton, Judy, *Scottish Myths and Legends*, 2003.

Kinninmonth, Sheila, *Fife Folk Tales*, 2017.

Marwick, Ernest, *An Anthology of Orkney Verse*, 1949.

Marwick, Ernest, *The Folklore of Orkney and Shetland*, 1975.

Mackenzie, Donald Alexander, *Wonder Tales from Scottish Myth and Legend*, 1917.

MacNab, Peter, *Tall Tales from an Island*, 1984.

MacPherson, George W., *Highland Myths & Legends*, 2001.

MacPherson, John, *Tales from Barra told by Coddie*, 1992.

Miller, Hugh, *Scenes and Legends of the North of Scotland*, 1831.

Muir, Tom, *The Mermaid Bride and Other Orkney Folk Tales*, 1998.

Muir, Tom, *Orkney Folk Tales*, 2014.

Nic Leodhas, Sorche, *Twelve Great Black Cats*, 1972.

Pegg, Bob, *Highland Folk Tales*, 2012.

Scottish Fairy Tales, Braken Books, 1993.

Smith, Gregor Ian & MacGregor, Alasdair Alpin, *Strange Stories and Folk Tales of the Highlands and Islands*, 1995.

Stephen, Ian, *Western Isles Folk Tales*, 2014.

Temperley, Alan, *Tales of the North Coast*, 1977.

Tulloch, Lawrence, *The Foy*, 2006.

Tulloch, Lawrence, *Shetland Folk Tales*, 2014.

Williamson, Duncan & Linda, *The Thorn in the King's Foot*, 1987.

Williamson, Duncan, *Tales of the Seal People*, 1992.

https://folklorescotland.com/the-vengeful-mermaid

'The De'il of Ardrossan', Folklore Scotland, folklorescotland.com/the-deil-of-ardrossan

https://whirlpool-scotland.co.uk/legend

And to all the storytellers, past and present, who I have learned stories from and whose versions of tales and whose inspiration is contained within this book.

The Scottish Storytelling Centre is delighted to be associated with the *Folk Tales* series developed by The History Press. Its talented storytellers continue the Scottish tradition, revealing the regional riches of Scotland in these volumes. These include the different environments, languages and cultures encompassed in our big wee country. The Scottish Storytelling Centre provides a base and communications point for the national storytelling network, along with national networks for Traditional Music and Song and Traditions of Dance, all under the umbrella of TRACS (Traditional Arts and Culture Scotland). See www.scottishstorytellingcentre.co.uk for further information. The Traditional Arts community of Scotland is also delighted to be working with all the nations and regions of Great Britain and Ireland through the *Folk Tales* series.

Donald Smith
Director, Tracs
Traditional Arts and Culture Scotland